Fitz Randolph

Traditions, a Genealogy and Family History of a Thousand Years

By L. V. F. Randolph

Life Member of the New Jersey Historical Society

Published by Pantianos Classics

ISBN-13: 978-1-78987-277-4

First published in 1907

Middleham Castle in 1780

In the year of Grace 1900 the writer of this book, venturing a volume of verses, dedicated his modest venture to the best of good women. It is especially suitable that this Story of a Thousand Years should be inscribed to that some delightful companion, inasmuch as she shared the fun and the fatigue of the journeyings in search of the fathers whose progenitorship and progress constitute the excuse and apology for this record.

Contents

Foreword vi

Story in Brief of a Thousand Years xi

Chapter One - Origin of the Name; Its Early Associations and Significance 12

Chapter Two - The Family in Early English Times and Its Descent through Lines of Nobility and Royalty 17

Chapter Three - The Family at Middleham and at Spennithorne. The Kinship to Ravensworth and the Friendship to Wycliffe 25

Chapter Four - Sifting Names and Relationships, & Considering Norman Character - Its Religious Predilections & its Noblest Production, George Washington 32

Chapter Five - Middleham Castle and Some of its Occupants 41

Chapter Six - From Yorkshire to Nottinghamshire and Back, with a Short Study in Heraldry 51

Chapter Seven - Kirkby, Sutton and Langton Hall 62

Chapter Eight - The Fitz Randolph House as Conjoined with the Westmoreland House 67

Chapter Nine - Review of Line of Descent from Rolf the Norseman to Edward the Pilgrim 76

Chapter Ten - Fitz Randolph Principles and Later Fortunate Alliances 79

Foreword

To the man of affairs genealogy and poetry are alike forbidden fruit. Yet, occasionally, one has been found bold enough to intimate that a little poetry would prove not only harmless but helpful to the poor human dray-horse of commerce or law, of finance or manufactures. And, again, as to doubtful indulgences, if one has religiously abstained both from whist and whisky until he has attained the life-limit of the Psalmist, he may perhaps at about the age of seventy take now and then a moment of comfort in either. Old-fashioned whist has been spoken of as an allowable dissipation of the aged, and, perhaps a like remark may be made concerning genealogy. A young man has no business with it whilst really important duties call and await attention. Besides, to the young, it leads the way to a habit of mendacity — or, at least, of romancing — such as might prove destructive to business morals and reputation. But against this temptation age opposes a settled character and sense of responsibility; and the old man may measurably be trusted to find the truth and to tell it — if upon reflection he finds it best to tell anything. A famous American wit, descanting upon the importance of early education, has hinted that we cannot begin the work too early, and that it is well to begin education at least so far back as to secure the well-considered birth of one's grandparents. It was, I think, one of the same type of self-complacent Boston Brahmins who indulged the presumption that a well-born man of the old Massachusetts stock would never have occasion to be born again. Without giving the least countenance to such a claim, one might hold excusable a certain consciousness of an early and long and valuable "education" on the part of a scion of a stock which had participated in the development of the ever-to-be reverenced Colonial character, and which had, prior to the Colonial period, been transplanted out of soil from which during many centuries great souls and deeds had grown. A just satisfaction and pride in the progress of American democracy is distinctly in accord with a sentiment of respect toward the far-away ancestry of Normandy and of Greater and Minor Brittany, whose strength, courage and achievements in mediaeval times went far toward rendering possible the civilization, enlightenment and freedom enjoyed by us now in such ample measure.

    The author is under obligation to many kind hearts, well-informed minds, and willing hands, for aid in furnishing facts herein contained. In the Motherland he and his companion were most hospitably entertained and efficiently assisted in their researches. The authorities of the British Museum at London, and of the Bodleian Library at Oxford, as well as of the libraries at York and Nottingham and Exeter, were attentive and generous to their wants. Many facts were gathered in conversation and correspondence with church officers and with other influential and intelligent gentlemen, and the assistance derived from perusing such rare and valuable works as those of Dugdale, Thoroton, Drake, Gale, Banks, Walker, and Speight (all of whom have paid much respect to the fathers herein mentioned), was beyond value. At home he has been indebted not a little to his revered friend, Hugh Vail of Santa Barbara, Cal. (now deceased), and to that accomplished genealogist and self-denying and industrious philanthropist, Oliver B. Leonard, of Plainfield, N. J. — whose ancestor participated with Nathaniel Fitz Randolph in the movement which gave to Princeton College a local habitation, and whose esteemed wife is an heir to all the Fitz Randolph traditions.

Where the writer has found differences existing between accredited antiquarians and historians on subjects of no vital importance to the aim of his narrative, he has adapted his recitals to the information or opinions advanced by those whose research has seemed the most thorough. As to certain matters he has quoted from differing authorities. For example, in reproducing the quaint plate from Drake's Eboracum, he has, in keeping with the picture and with the language of the conveyance of lands from William to Alan (as quoted by Drake), brought forward such statements and inferences as Drake and Dugdale and others have made to the effect that Alan Rufus was the same person as Alan Fergant, and that he was both nephew and son-in-law to William the Conqueror. According to Gale, however, we would be led to believe that these two names represent two distinct persons — that Alan Fergant, the son of a certain personage named Hoel, did marry William's daughter, Constance, but that Alan Rufus was William's important side-partner, and that, though a near kinsman of the Conqueror, he was neither his nephew nor his son-in-law.

In my own modest narrative, and in the diagram and outline given at the end of this prefatory chapter, I venture to prefer Gale's lines to Dugdale's, and even to so important and accurate an authority as Hume, who, on page 163 of the first volume of his History of England, tells us in effect that the great Alan, who joined the invading William with a large force of fighting men, was the son of Hoel and grandson of Conan, Puke of Brittany; and several encyclopedic and historical writers have fashioned their records, as to the facts here involved, on Hume's model.

In the course of preparing his book the writer has come into the rare good fortune of owning a well-preserved copy of Roger Gale's Honoris de Richmond. Influenced by an old tradition that Gale had, two hundred years ago, outlined the family history, he had sought the book throughout

England with the same zest evinced by John Burroughs in his pursuit of the nightingale through that delightful country, and it had evaded him. After much search he was by special permission permitted to have a few pages transcribed from a copy of the book possessed by an old library. When at last a singular opportunity was offered for acquiring ownership of the valued volume, he gladly availed of it, and has studied diligently this universally respected authority. It is in demi-folio form, well printed — partly in colors — and contains some beautiful engravings. No small part of its clear Latin text has reference to the facts and lines of the Fitz Randolph family.

The "foreword" is not infrequently the last word. The author finds, perhaps, on his hands, after completing his book, a residue of unassorted facts, and, possibly, of piquant suggestions, and these he gathers up and scatters about what professes to be the threshold of his volume, much in the same way in which our fishermen of the New Jersey coast — when they are "chumming" for bluefish — fling about their bait promiscuously in order to lure the fish worth catching to the vicinity of the catchers. To an indictment of this character the writer of this book might plead guilty — with reservations. The larger part of this prefatory chapter was written in advance of the book. As to any attempt at "piquancy," the writer should be in advance shriven of guilt — as touching a little work, much of whose material must of necessity consist of such records and paragraphs as "Abraham begat Isaac, and Isaac begat Jacob, and Jacob begat Joseph and his brethem." Concerning "unassorted facts," the writer confesses that he has still on hand a considerable supply, and he takes to himself at least this credit — that he has not burdened his readers with them. Not that they are devoid of interest, for they serve in various ways to buttress his thought and statements, but the narrative is sufficiently complete without them, and so they are withheld. One or two occur to him in writing these lines, and may be merely mentioned.

Reference is made in the course of the narrative to the *religious* thought and position of the family of Edward the Pilgrim. It may be well to emphasize the statement that they were not Puritans, though to some extent they were in sympathy with the Puritan position as differing with the religious autocracy established by Henry VIII. Still, for about a hundred years, reaching from the assumption by Henry of the control of England's ecclesiastical establishment to the departure from England of Edward the Pilgrim, these Fitz Randolphs were part and parcel of Henry's church. This appears in the church records at Sutton and at Kirkby, and in various other ways; and the writer has been privately favored with a copy of a record concerning a certain dispute as to pew rights which arose in Tudor times between the family of Christopher Fitz Randolph and the noble and distinguished ancestors of Colonel William Langton Coke. A decision on this question was rendered in the ecclesiastical courts, and mention of it can only be of interest here as confirming the religious affiliations of Christopher's family at that time. If a man in those days desired to live at all in England or to have any peace in living, and, especially, if he were a person of gentle birth, then the necessity arose (and it could hardly be escaped from) to remain a member of the church which had been thus established. There seems little reason to doubt, however, that the Fitz Randolphs had preferred to remain in the old Catholic communion — though the enterprise and liberality of their thought had longed for a larger liberty. Disallowing the alleged Puritanism of our ancestor, Edward the Pilgrim, I may add that he had not become a "dissenter" in the ordinary sense of that word for some time after his arrival at Cape Cod. It was seven years after he reached Massachusetts before he joined the Dissenting, or Pilgrim, Church at Barnstable, and that act was closely associated with his happy alliance with the family of Blossom, who had long been both dissenters and pilgrims.

One other "unassorted" fact may be just mentioned here. The writer remembers how from boyhood he was puzzled at the derivation of certain names of the early New Jersey hamlets. He learned later that the old settlement near the mouth of the Raritan was called Piscataway in a somewhat careless imitation of the name of the New England town, Piscataqua. One other name puzzled him still more, and that was the name of Totown, or Towtown. This last name has persisted to the present day. It must have been conferred upon the little hamlet to which it attached by the descendants of those sixteenth century Westmorelands whose ancestors had bravely fallen in the Lancastrian cause in the disastrous battle of Towton in 1461, and thus had left records of honor and of noble courage which their later descendants have been glad by any means, however humble, to perpetuate. Towton was really the turning point in the fratricidal strife known as the "Wars of the Roses." To suggest something of a parallel in our own day, Gettysburg may be mentioned. The great contest continued afterward, but almost without hope of ultimate success to the party then vanquished. King Edward IV had, after a desperate and bloody battle, beaten the sixty thousand soldiers arrayed against him by Queen Margaret, and she had fled away northward (as the Confederates fled southward after Gettysburg), and had left upon the lost field thirty-six thousand of her slain. Amongst the fallen were the Earls of Westmoreland and Northumberland, Sir John Neville and Lord Dacres — the first being then at the head of the family whose history is somewhat followed in our book, and the three others here mentioned being close kinsmen and compatriots in the Lancastrian cause. No wonder that the descendants of these great Earls should be proud of their courage, honor and patriotism as displayed on the sanguinary field of Towton.

The writer follows, in his final recapitulation and detailed facts of descent, Dr. E. A. Freeman's lines from the conquest of Normandy by Rolf to the conquest of England by William I, and Roger Gale's lines from Geoffrey of Brittany to Thomas, Edward, Christopher, Randolph and Cuthbert — and for the rest, the church register and mural tablet and the records of Thoroton, Blackner, Vail and Nathaniel Fitz Randolph.

This book is far from being a latter-day genealogy. The bit of patchwork at the end may serve as an example of what can readily be done — and doubtless better — by anyone else who will take the trouble to inquire about his heredity, and who will paste on paper the facts ascertained, from right to left; that is, toward the earlier generations. The writer lacks precise data of other personal or local lines, and possesses no fund of particular information such as would be useful to any other member of the family in tracing his own lineage forward from the Pilgrim Edward of Nottinghamshire. This fact he regrets, for he would gladly be of further service. Having traced his own line to Pilgrim progenitors, and having gathered substantial facts as to collateral connections, he has then continued to follow the threads to their early sources. All the Fitz Randolphs of the United States are descended from Edward of Nottinghamshire. In this fact rests the chief possibility of interest possessed by this book to any Americans who may now bear the name, or to any who have come of this stock.

If the information with care collected and herein collated can be relied on, and if such deductions and inferences as the writer has made are reasonable, then the following general outline may fairly represent a Story of a Thousand Years.

Story in Brief of a Thousand Years

Rolf
The Norseman, who conquered Normandy in the year 912 A.D.
|
William "Longsword"
Duke of Normandy, Died 948.
|
Richard, surnamed "The Fearless"
Reigned in Normandy fifty years. Died 996.
|
Richard, surnamed "The Good"
Reigned in Normandy thirty years. Died 1026. Richard's sister Emma married in the year 1002, Aetheired, the Saxon King of England. After his death she married the Danish King Cnut. His children were Richard, Duke of Normandy, whose wife was Judith, and a daughter Avicia, who married Geoffrey, Duke of Brittany.

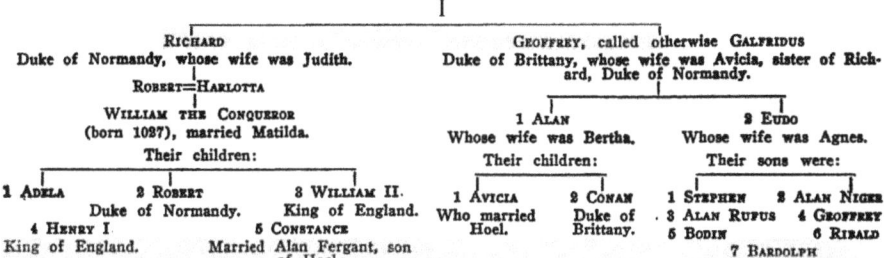

Alan Rufus was the close associate of William the Conqueror. He and Alan Niger and Bodin died without issue and the issue of the fourth son Geoffrey did not persist. Of the other sons of Eudo, Stephen was ancestor of an important line of Dukes and Princes. From Bardolph descended the Lords of Ravensworth, and the lineage whose most noble culmination was George Washington. Ribald was Lord of Middleham in Yorkshire, Eng. He was the father of Randolph and grandfather of Robert Fitz Randolph, who (through his mother), was grandson of the first Robert Bruce, and who built the Castle of Middleham about the year 1190. From the two sons of Robert ("Ranulph" and "Radulph") have descended, as we are led to believe, many royal personages, and also the Fitz Randolphs of Spennithorne and of Nottinghamshire of the 13th to the 17th centuries, as well as the Fitz Randolphs of Massachusetts and New Jersey of the 17th to the 20th centuries.

L. V. F. R.

Chapter One - Origin of the Name; Its Early Associations and Significance

The absence of church records, and the slenderness of most sorts of public records, prior to the year 1537, create a portion of the difficulty encountered in tracing early English family history. This difficulty is not a little augmented (in the endeavor to follow a kinship earlier than the sixteenth century) in the fact that the surnames were more or less shifting from generation to generation. Amongst the common people surnames, or family names, scarcely existed at all. When men were dependents, or servants, or serfs, they were lucky enough to have one name, even though that were sometimes only a nickname. Among the nobles the distinctive title, or lordship, was the thing whose persistence was desired and hoped for. This title, or lordship, descended in a line of primogeniture. Possibly in the younger and collateral branches a surname would persist for successive generations; but, even then, it might not descend in perpetuity.

A few of the old Norman names have been handed down marked by the Norman-French prefix "Fitz." [1] Among these is the name Randolph. [2] Like many other names of the earlier and less accurate ages it had several forms or phases. It was of Norse origin, and, in one or more of its forms, was known to the Danes, who were in the Middle Ages a vigorous, warlike and aggressive nation. Among the descendants of the Danes we find the name "Rauf." This was a modification of Rolf; and its later form, Ralph, came to be used as an abbreviation of certain longer forms of the same name, such as Randolph, Randolle, Randolffe, Ranulph, Rudolph and Randall. All these, and others, and the monosyllabic style as well, are used interchangeably as relating to the same person (or to the same family) by the historians, antiquarians and authorities on heraldry of the seventeenth and eighteenth centuries, upon whose information we largely depend in our endeavors to trace family lines and history. There appear to be two rather dissimilar original meanings to this ancient Norse name — one meaning is Hero, the other is Big Wolf. [3]

The name, in its ampler form or forms, was brought to England by the Norman conquerors in the latter half of the eleventh century, and was used, first, as the simple name of an individual, and afterwards as designating a continuing family. The first use of the name in England was in close connection with the family of William the Conqueror himself, and it will be noted that Rolf, the great Norse Chieftain was William's ancestor. In bringing forward this connection, we will therefore take a step backward to the parent trunk from which sprung the stem which became intertwined and engrafted not only with the Conquering Norman but also with his descendants and with several leading families of England, whose scions developed from ancient Saxon, Danish and Pictish stock.

The first prominent character who bore the name was the Viking leader Rolf, who was born about A.D. 860, and who died in 932. He made himself independent of Harold of Norway, visited Scotland, England and Flanders in his various expeditions, and about the year 912 established himself in what is now known as northern France, and became the first Duke of Normandy. His own name has also undergone some variations in history. Sometimes he is called Rollo [4] (the Latin form), and again Rou (the French form), and it would appear that the town of Rouen in northern France was named for him. This Scandinavian (and sometime pagan) invader embraced Christianity, but this did not deter him from pursuing his vocation as a warrior. From the first of his lodgment in France he was involved in the controversies which were in progress between the French princes and dukes. Upon his professing Christianity, he took the name of Robert from the Duke of the French, who acted as his godfather; but he was still generally spoken of by his Norse name.

His son and successor was William, surnamed "Longsword," who became the right-hand man of King Charles of France in 927, and reigned in Normandy until 943. William's son and successor was Richard "the Fearless," and it was during his long reign of half a century that the Duchy of France was united with the Western Kingdom, and the great combination was made of the High Dutch, Low Dutch, French and Aquitanian elements. Richard the Fearless died A.D. 996. His son was Richard "the Good," who reigned thirty years and kept an unbroken friendship between Normandy and France. He would have none but gentlemen about him, and in fact established a nobility which became permanent. His sister, Emma, in the year 1002, married Aethelred, the Saxon King of England, and this marriage was the first link in the chain of events that led to the Norman Conquest of England.

After Aethelred's death and the establishment in England of the Dane Cnut, Emma married Cnut. The son and successor of Richard the Good was a third Richard who reigned only two years, to 1028, and still kept up the French alliance. This Richard had a sister, Avicia, who married Geoffrey (sometimes called Galfridus), Duke of Brittany, and his posterity forms the chief subject of this book. In the same line, and after this third Richard, came Robert, who fell into difficulties with Cnut (whose sister he married and put away), and attempted an invasion of England on behalf of the children of Aethelred and Emma. He died in 1035 in the course of a pilgrimage to Jerusalem, and his son William, then a child of eight years, and known as William the Bastard, set out on his career to become William the Conqueror.

The people of Brittany were of Celt origin, but the Conquering Normans overran it, and the rulers were largely of Norman blood. The Dukes of Brittany and of Normandy had for generations maintained close relations. When they were not quarreling they were more or less intermarrying. Eudo of Brittany, son of Galfridus, or Geoffrey, joined hands and forces with his kinsman, William, and sent his son Alan, or Alain, to assist William in his English enterprise with a body of five thousand Bretons.

In "Notes from the Baronage of England in Saxon Time to Norman Conquest" by William Dugdale (London, 1675, Tome I. Page 46 to 53), we read as follows:

"Alan, first Earl of Richmond, son to Eudo, Earl of Brittany in France, came to England with Duke William of Normandy, commanded the rear of his army at Hastings. In his youth not a little famous for his valor, insomuch as he feared not the heroic spirited William, then Duke of Normandy, who challenged his right to Brittany. He married Constance, one of William the Conqueror's daughters, but died without issue. [5] He had four brothers, *Alanus Niger,* who also died without issue, another brother *Stephen,* who (one after another) succeeded to the Earldom of Richmond, and *Ribald, Lord* of Middleham, and *Bardulf,* whose son Akar was the founder of Josevaulz, an Abbey of the Cestercian Order in this Northern Tract. Ribald had by gift from his brother Alan, Middleham, together with Scrastone, Speningetorpe, Havogswell and Wadles. His son, Ralph, succeeded him. His wife, Agatha, was daughter to Robert de Brus of Skelton, and had with her the Lordship of Ailewic in Hertness." ...

"To Robert succeeded Ranulph his son and heir, who in 13 Joh. was acquitted from the Scutage of Scotland. He was buried at Coverham, leaving issue Ralphe his son, commonly called Raphe Fitz-Ranulph. Raphe was summoned with other eminent men of the North to go with Horse and Arms and 'all the power he could make' to march into Scotland for rescue of the King of that Realm, who had married a daughter of Henry IH, out of the hands of his rebellious subjects."

These details are given here partly by way of connecting the name of the first Rolf, or Ralf (or Rauf, or Ranulph, or Randolph), of Scandinavian leadership, with the name and descent as we find it in Northern England soon after the successful invasion of William the Conqueror and of his allies of the family of Eudo. It will be seen that it was the blood of these brave Norsemen (more or less recrossed, inbred and intermingled) that has descended through the lines of British kings and noble families.

Photograph, from Drake's Eboracum, of the Quaint and Ancient Drawing, Representing William the Conqueror in the Act of Delivering to His Nephew and Son-in-law Alan the Muniments of Title to Middleham and Other Important English Properties. These Properties Subsequently Passed into the Possession of Ribald, Brother of Alan and Grandfather of Robert Fitz Randolph, Lord of Middleham in the Twelfth Century.

We pause again in our narrative here to introduce the *form* of conveyance of the northern English properties made by William the Conqueror to Alan. This is copied from the quaint and valuable work by Francis Drake, Gent, F. R. S., published in 1736, entitled *Eboracum:*

"Ego Gulielmus, cognomine Bastardus, [6] do et concedo tibi Alano, nepoti meo, Britanic comiti, et heredibus tuis in perpetuum, omnes illas villas et terras, que nuper fuerent comitis Edwini in Eborascinia; cum foedis militum et ecclesius, et aliis libertatibus et confuetudinibus, ita libere et honozifice ficut idem Edwinus ea tenuit.

"Dat in oblidione cozam civitate Eboraci."

On the page in Drake's Eboracum opposite the narrative of the capture of the City of York by William and his allies, is a curious plate representing William in the act of handing over to the kneeling Alan the important document conveying to him the ownership of this immense domain.

The author of "Romantic Richmondshire," referring to this enormous gift made by William the Conqueror to Alan, speaks of the property as consisting of "no fewer than 440 manors and 140 knights' fees, besides many other bounties and privileges, which earned for him sometimes the title of Prince of the East Angles. His territorial possessions alone were probably not far short of 100,000 acres, and they were amongst the fairest in England. It is, however, not quite clear why the Conqueror should bestow all this wealth on a single one of his followers, and we can only surmise that some arrangement was made between William and the martial Count, his cousin, [7] or perhaps with his father, that, in the event of victory attending the invasion of England, and for the aid rendered by the Count, whose well-drilled regents are said to have numbered fully one-third of the Conqueror's army, these lands and honors were to be bestowed."

Alan died without issue, and of the English lands received by him — flying largely and chiefly in the northern counties of England — he gave to his brother Ribald certain estates which had belonged to Ghilpatric, the Dane, whose home and camp had been, prior to the Conquest, upon an eminence overlooking Middleham in Yorkshire. These estates were Middleham, Bolton, Spennithorne, Thornton, Watlass, and four others.

[1] Signifying "son of."

[2] It is something of a pity that with some of the Fitz Randolphs the argument of convenience has prevailed, leading them to drop the beginning portion of their name and thus creating confusion with the more numerous Kentish and American family of Randolphs. The writer himself may have been at fault all his life in compromising on the initial F, as many others have done, in lieu of using the complete and significant prefix "Fitz."

[3] The seeming dissimilarity partly recedes upon recalling the fact that courage and fierceness were nearly allied in the heroic conception of an age in which the right to conquer was regarded as inherent in one who had the might.
[4] At the end of the 10th "book," or division, of Bulwer's "Last of the Barons," he introduces his reader to "The illuminated hall of Edward, where the table was spread for the royal repast, and...from the gallery raised aloft, the musicians gave forth the rough and stirring melody which had gradually fallen out of usage, but which was once the Norman national air, and which the warlike Margaret of Anjou had retaught her minstrels — **The Battle Hymn of Rollo.**"
[5] It will have been noted that Gale differs with Dugdale about some of these particulars, holding that it was Alan Fergant, another kinsman of William, and not "Alan, first earl of Richmond, son to Eudo," who married Constance. This difference is not highly important to us. In general, we adopt Gale's lines. But the old plate, representing the gift of the land titles to Alan, taken from Drake's Eboracum (and also appearing in Gale's Registrum) seems to bear out the statements of Drake and Dugdale.
[6] As to William's parentage see also Hume's History of England, Vol. I, p. 152. He rejoiced in his "cognomen."
[7] Speight appears to agree with Gale as to the degree of relationship.

Chapter Two - The Family in Early English Times and Its Descent through Lines of Nobility and Royalty

In his old age Ribald entered the convent or abbey of St. Mary's, York, [1] and died about 1131, leaving three sons, namely, Ralph, or Randolph (his heir), Hervey and Henry. Randolph married Agatha, daughter of Robert De Bruis. His son, Robert, commonly known as Lord Robert Fitz Randolph, commenced to build the castle at Middleham, A.D. 1190.

Robert had three sons, the second of whom was called Randolph Fitz Robert or Randolph Fitz Randolph. Robert's wife was Helewisa, daughter of Ralph de Glenville. She, after Robert's death, founded Coverham Abbey.

Ralph (or Randolph) Fitz Randolph married Margery, the daughter of Robert Bigot, Duke of Norfolk, leader among the great barons who forced the Magna Charta from King John. Randolph died in 1251 and was buried in Coverham Abbey. His son, Ralph (or Randolph) Fitz Randolph (whose wife was Anastasia, daughter of William, Lord Percy) founded the Grey Friars at Richmond, Yorkshire, and died in 1270, leaving three daughters.

ST. MARY'S ABBEY, YORK.

To this Abbey Ribald, Lord of Middleham (grandfather of Robert Fitz Randolph) retired toward the close of his life in the early part of the twelfth century. Of the Abbey Church Ralph Adams Cram, author of the work entitled "The Ruined Abbeys of Great Britain" (published 1905) enthusiastically writes, characterizing it as "The most beautiful church in England, and one of the most perfect examples of consummate architecture in the Christian world."

It is known that the Castle of Middleham, built by Robert Fitz Randolph, passed into the possession of Robert Neville, who married Mary, eldest of the three daughters [2] of the last-mentioned Randolph Fitz Randolph; and the descendants of Robert Neville and Mary Fitz Randolph have filled the foremost places in English history. Their blood has come down to our day in the veins of all the Plantagenet, Tudor, Stuart and Guelph sovereigns of England (always excepting Henry VII, the first Tudor king, who seized the crown on a pretense), and the same Fitz Randolph blood is commingled in nearly all the important royal families of Continental Europe. Entering through Richard Plantagenet (who married the great, great, great granddaughter of Mary Fitz Randolph of Middleham) the lineage includes Edward IV, Richard III, Edward V and his sister Elizabeth, the queen of Henry VII. A few details are given below, including a review of a few facts already mentioned. These are gathered from various historical authoriti.es — including Green's History of England, Hume's History of England, Gairdner's House of Lancaster, British Cyclopedia, Vol. 14, page 257, J. P. Pritchett's "Works of the Nevilles" and "Account of Middleham Castle and Church," and the works of Dugdale, Banks and other writers.

Robert Fitz Randolph built the Castle of Middleham, A.D. 1 190. His wife was Helewisa de Glanville.

Their son Randolph [3] Fitz Randolph (sometimes called Ralph Fitz Robert) married Margery, the daughter of Robert Bigot, the Duke of Norfolk. This was an important alliance. Roger Bigot (or Bigod) was Constable of Norwich Castle, one of the founders of Norwich Cathedral, and one of the first great leaders to protest against absolute Papal domination in England. His seal and that of his son are found on the exemplification of Magna Charta, which he was largely instrumental in obtaining for the English people from King John; and both he and his son were numbered among the twenty-five barons who then controlled the sovereignty of England.

The son of Randolph and Margery was Ralph (or Randolph) Fitz Randolph who married Anastasia, daughter of William, Lord Percy, [4] and died about 1269.

Their daughter, Mary Fitz Randoph, married (about 1260) Robert Neville, Lord of Raby, lineally descended from Uchtred, the great Saxon Earl of Northumberland and his wife, Elfgiva, daughter of King Ethelred II. Robert Neville died in 1271. His wife died in 1320.

Their only son was Ralph (or Randolph) the first Lord Neville, who was summoned to the House of Lords by Edward I in the famous Parliament of Lincoln called in the year 1301. He died in the fifth year of Edward HI, that is A.D. 1332. His first wife was Euphemia, daughter of John Qavering. Their only child, Robert, died childless in 1318. His first wife having died also, he married Margery, daughter of Marmaduke Thweng, and they had one son, Ralph or Randolph, who was the hero of the Battle of Neville's Cross in 1346. This Randolph enlarged the Castle of Middleham in 1400. He died in the forty-first year of Edward III, that is A.D. 1368. His wife was Alicia, daughter of Hugo de Audley, and their only son was John (de Neville) who participated with his father in the glory and the gain of Neville's Cross, conducting the negotiation by which the Scottish King David, captured at that battle, was ransomed for a large sum. John married for his first wife Mathilde de Percy, [5] and for his second wife Elizabeth daughter and heir of Lord Latimer, of Danby. He died A.D. 1389. The posterity of the second wife's children appears to have come to an end in the next generation. By the first wife John had a son, Randolph, who was by Richard II in the year 1397 created Earl of Westmoreland. Randolph of Westmoreland was a vigorous, able man who lived until the year 1435. He had two wives by whom he had about an even score of children, nearly all of whom became titled and powerful. His large estates were principally divided between the eldest son by the first marriage (who, of course, became Earl of Westmoreland) and the eldest son by the second marriage, who became the great Earl of Salisbury and Warwick (whose more famous son, the Earl of Warwick, was known as "Warwick the Kingmaker"), having the Yorkshire estates of Middleham and Sheriff-Hutton.

The first of the two wives of Ralph or Randolph de Neville, Earl of Westmoreland, was Margaret, Lady Stafford, a descendant of King Edward I, and the second wife was Joan of Beaufort, daughter of John of Gaunt, who was a son of Edward III.

For the moment we defer specific attention to the line descending from Randolph, Duke of Westmoreland, by his first wife. Lady Stafford, and proceed with the notable line of descent from Randolph and his second wife, Joan of Beaufort. By this wife he had amongst other children, a daughter named Cicely, who was called "The Rose of Raby," [6] who married Richard Plantagenet, Duke of York, who was slain at the battle of Wakefield in 1460.

In view of the fact that the line of Nevil, or Westmoreland, enters so largely into the warp and woof of this narrative, we interrupt here the genealogical details above commenced to insert a few lines from the 283d and 284th pages of the second volume of Hume's History of England touching the character and record of Richard Plantagenet and the circumstances of his alliance with the Nevil [7] family:

"Richard was a man of valor and abilities, of a prudent conduct and mild disposition: he enjoyed an opportunity of displaying these virtues in the government of France; and though recalled from that command by the intrigues and superior interest of the Duke of Somerset, he had been sent to suppress a rebellion in Ireland, had succeeded much better in that enterprise than his rival in the defence of Normandy, and had even been able to attach to his person and family the whole Irish nation whom he was sent to subdue. In the right of his father he bore the rank first of prince of the blood; and by this station he gave lustre to his title derived from the family of Mortimer, which, though of great nobility, was equalled by other families in the kingdom, and had been eclipsed by the royal descent of the house of Lancaster. He possessed an immense fortune from the union of so many successions, those of Cambridge and York on the one hand, and those of Mortimer on the other; which last inheritance had before been augmented by a union of the estates of Clarence and Ulster with the patrimonial possessions of the family of March. *The alliances, too, of Richard, by his marrying the daughter of Ralph Nevil, Earl of Westmoreland, had widely extended his interest among the nobility, and had procured him many connections in that formidable order.*

"The family of Nevil was, perhaps, at this time the most potent, both from their opulent possessions and from the characters of the men, that has appeared in England. For, besides the Earl of Westmoreland and the Lords Latimer, Fauconberg, and Abergavenny, the Earls of Salisbury and Warwick were of that family, and were of themselves, on many accounts, the greatest noblemen of the kingdom. The Earl of Salisbury, brother-in-law to the Duke of York, was the eldest son, by a second marriage, of the Earl of Westmoreland, and inherited (by his wife, daughter and heir of Montacute, Earl of Salisbury, killed before Orleans) the possessions and title of that great family. His eldest son, Richard, had married Anne, the daughter and heir of Beauchamp, Earl of Warwick, who died Governor of France; and by this alliance he enjoyed the possessions, and had acquired the title of that other family, one of the most opulent, most ancient, and most illustrious in England. The personal qualities also of these two earls, especially of Warwick, enhanced the splendor of their nobility and increased their influence over the people. This latter nobleman, commonly known, from the subsequent events, by the appellation of the *King-maker*, had distinguished himself by his gallantry in the field, by the hospitality of his table, by the magnificence, and still more by the generosity, of his expense, and by the spirited and bold manner which attended him in all his actions. The undesigning frankness and openness of his character rendered his conquests over men's affections the more certain and infallible; his presents were regarded as sure testimonies of esteem and friendship, and his professions as the overflowings of his genuine sentiments. No less than thirty thousand persons are said to have daily lived at his board in the different manors and castles which he possessed in England; the military men, allured by his munificence and hospitality, as well as by his bravery, were zealously attached to his interests; the people in general bore him an unlimited affection; his numerous retainers were more devoted to his will than to the prince or to the laws; and he was the greatest, as well as the last, of those mighty barons who formerly overawed the crown and rendered the people incapable of any regular system of civil government."

Richard and Cicely had six children, namely. King Edward IV; Edmund, Earl of Rutland (who, with his father was slain at Wakefield); George, Duke of Clarence (who married Isabelle Neville, daughter of Warwick, the King-maker); King Richard III (who married his cousin, Ann Neville, second daughter of the great Warwick); Elizabeth (who married John de la Pole, Duke of Suffolk); and Margaret who married Charles, Duke of Burgundy.

The first of the above six children, Edward IV, had four children, namely: Edward V; Richard, Duke of York; Elizabeth (who married Henry VII); and Catherine, who married Sir William Courtenay.

Henry VII and his wife Elizabeth, just mentioned, had (in the male line) Henry VIII, who had (by his wives Catherine of Aragon, Anne Boleyn and Jane Seymour) children named Mary and Elizabeth and Edward, who all reigned and died without issue. Henry VII and his wife Elizabeth also had daughters, Margaret and Mary. Mary's granddaughter. Lady Jane Grey, was beheaded in 1554. Margaret married for her first husband James IV, King of Scots, and for her second husband, Archibald Douglas, Earl of Angus. The son of James IV was James V, whose daughter was Mary Stuart, Queen of Scots. The daughter of Margaret and Archibald Douglas was Margaret Douglas, who married Matthew Stuart, Earl of Lenox. Their first child was Henry Stuart, Lord Darnly, who married Mary, Queen of Scots, daughter of James V, as above, and their son was James I of England, who was also James VI of Scotland.

James I of England was the father of Charles I (born 1600, beheaded 1649, married Henrietta of France) and of Elizabeth (born 1596, died 1662), whose husband was Frederick, Elector of Palatine.

Charles I was the father of Charles II, and also of James II and of Mary, who married William, Prince of Orange. Mary and William were the parents of William III, who married his cousin Mary, — first daughter of James II and his first wife, Ann Hyde.

Elizabeth, daughter of James I, had a daughter Sophia, who married Ernest Augustus, Elector of Hanover. Their son was George I, King of England (born 1660, died 1727), who married Sophia Dorothea Zell.

Their son was George II (bora 1683, died 1760), who married Caroline of Brandenburg-Anspach. Their son was Frederick, Prince of Wales, born 1707, died 1751. His son was George III, born 1738, died 1820, married Charlotte, of Mecklenburg-Strelitz.

George and Charlotte had four children: George IV, William IV, Edward, Duke of Kent, and Ernest Augustus, King of Hanover. The line of English royalty has descended through Edward, Duke of Kent, and through Victoria, who was born in 1819, and who married Prince Albert of Saxe-Coburg and Gotha. Thus Edward VII, now King of England (son of Victoria), and all the English sovereigns reigning before him from Edward IV downward (excepting only Henry VII), have carried in their veins the blood of the Fitz Randolphs, all of them being descended from Robert Fitz Randolph, Lord of Middleham.

We have thus followed to some extent the descent of Ralph or Randolph (sometimes also called Ranulph), son of Robert Fitz Randolph, Lord of Middleham. Later on we shall see that Robert had *three* sons, only one of whom was childless, and *two* of whom had long lines of descent, and that the family of one of these dwelt long at Spennithorne near Middleham.

It has been seen that Ralph, or Randolph, son of Ribald and father of Robert Fitz Randolph, Lord of Middleham, married Agatha, daughter of Robert de Bruis (or de Bruce). This last-named Robert was the first Robert de Bruce, father of the distinguished line of eight Robert Bruces, and it is not amiss here to quote the resume of this line as given in the Encyclopaedia Britannica by Dr. Aeneas J. G. Mackay — this resume ending with King Robert, the hero and victor of Bannockburn.

'The first Robert de Bruce, a follower of William the Conqueror, was rewarded by the gift of many manors, chiefly in Yorkshire, of which Skelton was the principal. His son, the second Robert, received from David I, his comrade at the court of Henry I, a grant of the Lordship of Annandale; and his grandson, the third Robert, siding with David against Stephen at the battle of 'The Standard,' became a Scottish instead of an English baron. The fourth Robert married Isobel, natural daughter of William the Lion, and their son, the fifth Robert, married Isabella, second daughter of

Drawing from Page 99 of Appendix of "Honoris de Richmond," Representing the Seal of the First Robert Bruce

David, Earl of Huntingdon, niece of the same Scottish king."

"Robert, called The Bruce (1274-1329), King of Scotland, was the son of the seventh Robert de Bruce, Lord of Annandale in his own right, and Earl of Carrick in right of his wife Marjery...His grandfather, the sixth Robert de Bruce, claimed the crown of Scotland as son of Isabella, second daughter of David, Earl of Huntingdon; but Baliol, grandson of Margaret, eldest daughter, was preferred."

At Bannockburn, June 24, 1314, Bruce routed the army of Edward II, secured the independence of Scotland and confirmed his own title to the throne.

The chief author of Scottish independence [King Robert, the Bruce] barely survived his work. His last years had been spent chiefly at the Castle of Cardross; ...and the conduct of war, as well as the negotiations for peace, had been left to the young leaders, Randolph and Douglas, whose training was one of Bruce's services to his country."

It will be seen that Robert Fitz Randolph, Lord of Middleham, was grandson to the renowned head of the Bruce family, and that, not only in the veins of the British royal family, but also in the veins of the Fitz Randolphs of New Jersey (descendants of Robert Fitz Randolph of Middleham) still flows the blood of the Bruces.

[1] According to Gale, Ribald's childless brother Bodin went with him into monastic retirement.

[2] Dormant and Extinct Baronage of England by T. C Banks, London, 1807, Vol. I, page 165. Also see Baronage of England in Saxon Time to Norman Conquest by Wm. Dugdale, London, 1675, Tome 1. Bulwer Lytton says in "The Last of the Barons"— "Middleham Castle was built by Robert Fitz Ranulph, grandson of Ribald, younger brother of the Earl of Bretagne and Richmond, nephew to the Conqueror." The novelist here follows (in regard to the Kinship of Alan to William) the lines of Dugdale and Banks, differing somewhat from Gale's carefully drawn genealogical statements. The writer of this book brings forward the opinion entertained by Dugdale, Banks and Bulwer in exhibiting the quaint picture from Drake's Eboracum, but he inclines to Gale's opinion as probably more accurate.

[3] Randolph, or Ranulphus. or Ralph. He and others of this name are mentioned in various records and histories, sometimes under one style and again under another. As Henry and Harry and Hal are substantially one name, so are the various forms of the name Randolph, and they are so used in this book, the writer more frequently using the name Randolph as the admitted solvent and equivalent of others. In Gale's Latin "Registrum," on which great reliance is placed, the forms used in the records of the Fitz Randolphs, Nevilles and Westmorelands are Ranulphus and Radulphus.

[4] The Fitz Randolph blood has received a double injection of the blood of the great Percy family. Earls of Northumberland and Worcester. We have here the fact that the mother of Mary Fitz Randolph of Middleham was a Percy, and we shall see later that her great grandson joined in wedlock with one of this illustrious family. These two lines of kinship were much united in fortune and in feeling. They fought and fell together at Towton in the fifteenth century, and in the sixteenth they together essayed — bravely though fruitlessly — to withstand Tudor aggression.

[5] Here the blood of the Percies, Dukes of Northumberland and of Worcester again mingles with the Fitz Randolph blood — continuing so to do through subsequent generations and until our day. The father of Matilda (a descendant of William. Lord Percy, namely Lord Henry Percy) defended and protected John Wycliffe against the Archbishop of Canterbury.

[6] Pritchett remarks, "Nearly every royal family in Europe can trace its descent from the same noble and beautiful lady, called 'The Rose of Raby.'"

[7] We here follow Hume's spelling of the name Nevil. Other historians spell it Nevile, or more generally, Neville.

Chapter Three - The Family at Middleham and at Spennithorne. The Kinship to Ravensworth and the Friendship to Wycliffe

It is proposed to trace the detailed record of the English Fitz Randolph family, which removed to the New World about the year 1630, and to dwell somewhat on certain pivotal facts which occurred in Nottinghamshire about a hundred years earlier than the Pilgrimage. I am informed that an American gentleman, who has spent much effort in tracing the history of this Fitz Randolph family, of which he himself is a member, has ascertained to his own complete satisfaction that the American and Nottinghamshire line came down directly and distinctly from Lord Robert Fitz Randolph, the builder of the Castle of Middleham. I have not had access to his documents, or proofs; but in pursuing an independent and somewhat painstaking line of research I have been irresistibly led to a like conclusion. As to the reasonableness of this conclusion the reader is invited to judge.

Our American forebears, adopting cordially the broad doctrine of human equality, have made small insistence on descent from noble families — whose claims and views would have disallowed the democratic faith of their posterity. Moreover, the conditions of life into which the Pilgrim of the seventeenth century came were hard and engrossing. He and those who came after him for a century or more took scant interest in recurring to themes no longer practical and hardly congenial. Yet through all this, and adown the Fitz Randolph generations, ran a sentiment and a tradition going back to Langton Hall and to the Castle of Middleham, and to the ancient leaders of Normandy and Brittany. Occasionally as public journalism progressed, a printed article would appear bearing along this tradition. It has been an agreeable diversion to the writer, after half a century of struggling with practical and imminent duties, to trace this tradition to its early sources.

I am convinced that the family which lived in Nottinghamshire in the sixteenth century and in the early part of the seventeenth century, and which then emigrated to Massachusetts, and almost forty years later settled at Piscataway near the eastern coast of New Jersey, had its origin in the kinship associated with the great Earl Alan and his brothers whom I have mentioned (sons of Eudo of Brittany), and may in common with many great families in Europe claim as their ancestor the redoubtable Lord of Middleham.

The possibilities of the precise lines of descent from Alan's brothers, sons of Eudo, at first appear somewhat various. The name Fitz Randolph, used every now and then as a family name for successive generations, appears amongst ancient writings and registers in various though not in many places, and always apparently derived from, and having reference to, this particular group.

Notable examples are found in the very important book published in London in the year 1722 by Roger Gale, and entitled *Registrum Honoris de Richmond*, The material of this book is chiefly Latin, with copious extracts from "Domesday," and with interesting historical notes in ancient (or Norman) French. Its "appendix" and "observations," which comprise more than half of the splendid volume of about four hundred pages, are of special value to us in these family researches.

At page 247 we have an outline of descent of the Spennithome line of Fitz Randolphs extending through a period of upwards of three hundred years — Spennithome being on the other side of the river Yore from Middleham, and contiguous thereto, and for many generations the seat of a division of this family. The outline here begins with "Robertus, Dominus de Middleham" who, as has already been noted, married Helewisa de Glanville (or Glenville) and had three sons. The oldest of these, Walrannus, died without issue, leaving to the second son, Ranulphus, the Lordship. His progeny married, as has been seen, into the powerful family of the Nevilles and later on carried along the proprietorship of the Castle of Middleham into the royal family of England. The *third* son was *Radulphus;* but, as Gale informs us, he is in the record always called *Ranulphus.* The line as sketched by Gale will be found on following page.

This outline is interesting and suggestive to one bent on genealogical research, though it is confessedly incomplete, not only as to marriages but also as to progeny — particularly between the periods of Edward II and Edward IV. For the most part Gale has apparently only here brought forward the names of the heirs of the family property, or first-born sons. In this same valuable Registrum of Gale, under the heading — "Observationes in genealogiam comitum Richemondiae" (page 247, Appendix), we find the following note:

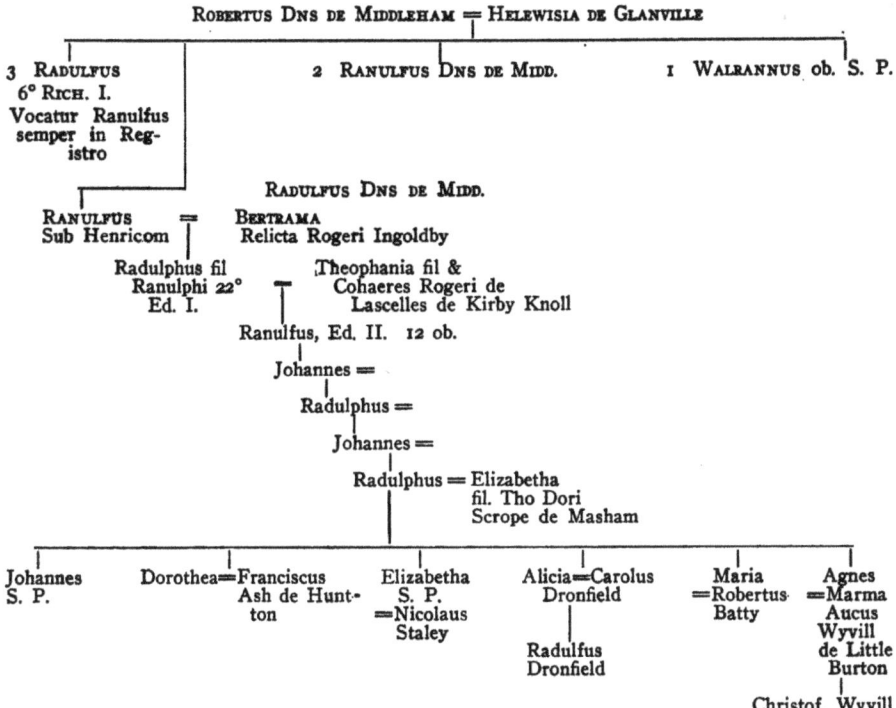

["P. 70. I. 5. Dominus Ranulphus filius Radulphi] Filius erat Ranulphus hie Radulphi, filii natu tertii Roberti Domini de Middleham & Helewisiae de Glanville, propatrui Mariae Dominae de Middleham, quae maximam patrimonii partem secum marito suo Roberto de Neville advexit: Prius autem Radulphus filius Roberti terras has Subtus in Registro enumeratas a patre suo obtinuerat, quas & Ranulpho filio demisit. Sedem suam apud Spennythom fixerunt, unde & prosapia eorum locupleti satis haereditate donata, nomine Fitz Randolphorum de Spennythorn multis ibi inclaruit annis, donec tandem deficiente masculina prole, cum filiabus ad alios bona abierunt."

The following is a fairly careful rendering from the formal Latin to the English of our day:

"Lord Ranulph Fitz Radulph — This Ranulph was the son of Radulph, third son of Robert, Lord of Middleham and of Helewisa de Glanville who [Radulph] was uncle of Mary, Countess of Middleham, who brought the largest part of her inheritance with her to her husband Robert de Neville. Before this, moreover, Radulph, son of Robert, had obtained from his father the lands enumerated in the register, which he handed down to his son Ranulph. They fixed their seat at Spennithorne, from which, under the name of the Fitz Randolphs of Spennithorne, their family, endowed with an inheritance of considerable wealth, increased in importance there for many years, until finally, through the death of male heirs, the property went with the daughters to others."

Taking another line of research, we find the following mention made (also in Gale's "Registrum") of Henry Fitz Randolph and of his son Hugh:

"Henry Fitz Randolf cy desoulx estoit tres noble Baron, & morust en Ian de grace Mil c c LXII & del regne de Roy Henry tierce XLIX, & est ensevely a Jorevaulx. Et Adam son frere est ensevely en la cymitere hors de Leglise illeoques."

"Ycesti Hugh Fitz Henry, frere & heir de Randolf desoulx escript, qi Randolf morust sanz issue de son corps, succeda en leritage apres Randolf son frere, & morust a Berewik sur Tese Ian de grace Mil c c c iiii, le iiii Ides du Marce & du Regne le Roy Edward primier xxii tost apres la siege & gaigne del Chastel du Stryvelyn en Escoce & fuit ensevely a Rumaldkirk le xi kalendes Davril, par John Priour de Giseburgh & sa femme Albrede morust a Hurworth sur Tese, & fuit a Jorevaux ensevely joust Monsire Henry Fitz Randolf pier du dit Hugh le viii kalendes de Fever Ian de grace Mil ccc ii."

It will be noted that the ancient record is here found to have been kept in (old) French. This has for convenience been rendered into English by the writer of this book, as follows:

"Henry Fitz Randolf here mentioned was a very noble lord and died in the year of grace 1262, and of the reign of King Henry III, the 49th, and is buried at Jervaulx Abbey. And Adam, his brother, is buried in the cemetery outside of the church there.

JERVAULX ABBEY: ENDOWED BY THE FITZ RANDOLPHS.
Now a Fascinating Ruin near Middleham in Yorkshire.

'This Hugh Fitz Henry, brother and heir of Randolf here below written (which Randolph died without issue of his body), succeeded to the inheritance after Randolph, his brother, and died at Berwick-on-Tees in the year of grace 1304 — the 4th of the Ides of March, and in the 22d year of the reign of King Edward the First, soon after the siege and capture of Sterling Castle in Scotland, and was buried at Romald-Kirk, the eleventh of the calends of April, by John, Prior of Guisborough, and his wife, Albreda, died at Hurworth-on-Tees, and was buried at Jervaulx, close to Monsire Henry Fitz Randolph, father of the said Hugh, on the 8th of the calends of February in the year of grace 1302."

It is doubtless this Henry Fitz Randolph to whom the author of "Romantic Richmondshire" refers in writing of the fascinating remains of Jervaulx Abbey, five miles from Middleham — "Here is a much mutilated effigy of a knight in link-mail, which, from the armorial bearings on the shield, has hitherto been regarded as a memorial to Henry, 4th Lord Fitz Hugh, who died in 1424. But from the character of the sculpture this is impossible. The monument is more than 100 years older than this date, and in all probability represents one of the Fitz Ranulphs, ancestors of the Fitz Hughs." The writer has seen this effigy and sorrowed over its exposure and ruin.

We then further ascertain by a study of the material furnished in this interesting and valuable "Registrum" that the father of this Henry Fitz Randolph married Alice, daughter and heiress to Adam of Stanely, Baron, who was descended in a noble line, comprising half a dozen generations, from the great Dane, Cospatrick, mentioned as a brave and distinguished leader by Hume and Scott and other historians, and who was at one time an ally, but for the most part was an enemy of the great Conquering William of Normandy. In this same line of Cospatrick occurs now and then, amongst other Danish names, that of Rauf. In this line also (and near of kinship to Alice, who married Randolph, the father of Henry Fitz Randolph), was Adam of Thoresby, who married Sibille, "daughter of Monsiere Randolf Fitz Randolf of Spennithorne." Following down the line of Henry Fitz Randolph, we find that he had one son, Randolf, who died without issue, and one other son, Hugh, whose wife's name was Albreda. Their only son was Henry, who married Eve, the daughter of Monsiere Bulmer. Only one son of theirs is mentioned (also of the name of Henry), who married Joan, or Johanne, daughter and heiress of the Chevalier Richard Fourneux. They in turn had two sons, only one of whom appears to have married; he, too, marrying a "Joan or Johanne," daughter of "Monsiere Henry Le Scroope de Mashan." This, in the Registrum, appears to be one of the mentionings of the great lordship of Scrope, whose participation in the history of the northern English counties had become so important. A still earlier close alliance of these two great kinships (coming down from Eudo and his brave sons) is mentioned thus by the author of Romantic Richmondshire — "In the reign of Edward I the Burton estate belonged to Sir Geoffrey le Scrope, the famous Chief Justice of Masham. The estate descended to Ralph Fitz Randolph of Spennithome by his marriage to Elizabeth, one of the three daughters, and co-heiress, of Thomas, Lord Scrope of Masham."

This later Henry and Joan had also a son who died without issue, and still another Henry who survived and married Elizabeth, daughter and sole heiress of Marmion and St. Quintin. [1] The children of Henry and Elizabeth were exceptionally numerous. Of these some died young. One appears to have been drowned in the river Humber. One, Rauf, went abroad and died in France; and it seems to be impossible to follow with certainty their various threads of descent (even Gale's lines concerning them are scanty and manifestly incomplete); but among them was one William, who married Margie, daughter of the noble St. William of Willoughby, and these appear to have had several children, amongst whom was a later Henry.

Richmondshire is full of pleasant and inviting bypaths — all having relation to the old Roman highway that ran through Middleham. And so the student of Fitz Randolph genealogy can hardly avoid turning aside now and then into some enticing vale of thought or research closely allied with his own theme. In Speight's charming book entitled "Romantic Richmondshire," in the chapter concerning Hipswell, he writes as follows:

"Proceeding from Colburn in the direction of Catterick Bridge you pass the site of another old-time hospital with chapel, which is said by Clarkson to have been founded by Henry Fitz Randolph, Lord of Ravensworth, in the time of Henry HI; but as the arms of Marmion are on the hospital seal, it is not unlikely that some member of that family was the true founder."

We have seen that a descendant of Lord Henry Fitz Randolph married Elizabeth, the sole heiress of the family of Marmion, and it is not unlikely that this is the solution of the difficulty suggested by Mr. Speight.

Immediately in the neighborhood indicated in the above quotation, at Hipswell, Yorkshire, and within a short distance of the frowning Keep of Richmond, was born about the year 1320 the great reformer, John Wycliffe, whose lineage was also of the ancient family celebrated by Scott in "Marmion." He it was who translated the Bible into English about the year 1380, and whose preaching against the doctrine of transubstantiation and in favor of a simple religion, binding man to his Maker without need of priestly mediation or sacraments, struck the highest note of clear protest against the prelatical rule of mediaeval times, and the one which really constituted the keynote of the progressive reformation that struggled toward success in the sixteenth and seventeenth centuries.

In two other respects do the work and record of John Wycliffe find suitable mention in this historic outline, and these additional reasons for reference to the great Reformer consist in two friendships of his — the one with the brave and powerful John of Gaunt, whose blood and descent commingle through the following ages with those of the Fitz Randolph line, and the other friendship being that of the Archbishop of Armagh, Richard Fitz Ralph. [2]

ANCIENT MINIATURE PORTRAIT
OF
JOHN WYCLIFFE.

This Fitz Ralph, in some of the earlier records called St. Richard, was Primate of all Ireland. Reference is made to him in an interesting book first printed in folio in Exeter in 1701, — a copy of which has the publication date of 1810. The writer found in a library of Exeter (of the institution opposite the cathedral) a book called "Worthies of Devon," — the author being one John Prince, Vicar of Berry Pomeroy. He says that this Fitz Ralph was "called by some Richardus Radulphi." [3] The author goes on to say "I find the family of Fitz Ralffe to have flourished in these parts from the Norman Conquest down to the days of King Edward I. They anciently called themselves Ralph the son of Ralph — the same as Fitz Ralph."

The author of this biographical sketch of the Archbishop goes on to narrate the circumstance of the education of his hero at Oxford, and the conduct of a campaign by him of courageous opposition to the mendicant friars, and to set forth the persecution which resulted from these events. The Archbishop presented his argument before Pope Innocent VI, but, as the author says, "he found the proverb true — 'reason does not always rule the roast.'"

We learn from other sources that Wycliffe had personally received in his youth the instruction of this Richard Fitz Ralph, or Fitz Randolph, Archbishop of Armagh, and had adopted, largely as a result of such instruction, the simple and intense faith which he held and preached, particularly as to the right of the individual soul to hold communion with its Maker, untrammeled by the interference of priest or friar.

[1] The family of St. Quintin received its name from the capital of Picardy, France, and attended William the Conqueror on his invasion of England. (Romantic Richmondshire, p. 157.) Among the knights who aid was commanded by King Edward III was Will St. Quintin (Vida Rot. Scot. 12th Ed. 3d, p. 529). His effigy is in Hornby ch., Yorkshire.

[2] A *third* friendship might also in this connection again be mentioned — namely, that which subsisted between John Wvcliffe and Lord Henry Percy, Earl of Northumberland, who protected Wycliffe when cited before the Archbishop at St. Paul's. A female descendant of this noble Earl married a descendant of the ancient Fitz Randolphs, namely the father of the first Earl of Westmoreland, and the Percy blood came doubly down to the Fitz Randolphs of Tudor times and later.

[3] Richard was a favorite name amongst the descendants of Akary Fitz Bardolph, as appears in Gale's elaborated lists. Wycliffe's instructor may easily nave been one of these, and thus related to the Lord of Ravensworth. It seems highly probable that he descended from Bardolph, son of Eudo, who had a considerable family, and who received large properties from his brother Bodin, when the last-named went into monastic retirement at St. Mary's, York.

Chapter Four - Sifting Names and Relationships, & Considering Norman Character - Its Religious Predilections & its Noblest Production, George Washington

The family lines in England, whose record we are endeavoring to follow, is beset with fewer doubts because of the relative infrequency of the recurrence of the name. The name has never been of wide use in English life. In the United States there are to-day many more Randolphs and Fitz Randolphs than there ever were in England. Examination of authorities found in the Bodleian Library at Oxford shows that Randolph was once a distinguished name in that university town. It still attaches to a reputable hostelry of Oxford, by which it was adopted from respect to two highly educated gentlemen, one of whom was there a professor of Greek and of Divinity, and the other (his father) was president of a college.

This family of Oxford distinction was for many generations domiciled in Kent, and produced in England several men of learning and repute; and it was from the same family that the Randolphs of Virginia became an offshoot in the seventeenth century.

In the history of the old city of Chester the name appears amongst the heroic leaders and rulers of that famous burg. The name is found now and then in the lists of mayors of great cities (London, Nottingham and others), and also in the lists of bishops of some of the great cathedrals. Sometimes it is in the more ancient lists in the single form of Radulph, or Ranulph, or Ralph, and again it will be found associated with some surname, or with another name prefixed. In each case it appears to stand as an indication of a Norman or Norse lineage, and is more or less traceable to Scandinavian origin.

The Fitz Randolphs are, in England, fewer than the Randolphs. Indeed, it is now scarcely possible to find there any representatives of the former name; and although it is probable that in the earlier centuries the relationship between them was a close one (all the original Randolphs and Fitz Randolphs being Normans or Norsemen), still the line, or lines, of Fitz Randolphs constitute a distinct subject and study, and the particular line of which this paper treats appears to have been continuous by itself in the Old World and the New for more than seven hundred years.

It has been seen that in Yorkshire the descent of the Lord of Middleham and of the Lord of Ravensworth intertwined at certain points, and that both branches came down from the before-mentioned sons of Eudo.

Mention is made by Dugdale and by Banks (in their books on the English baronages) of a certain Robert Fitz Randolph (or Robert Fitz Ranulph), who was Lord of Afreton, Norton, and Marnhan, in the time of King Henry II, and who was sheriff of the counties of Nottingham and Derby of the 12th, 13th, 14th, 15th, and half of the 16th year of that king's reign.

The same character is mentioned also in Blackner's History of Nottingham; and Blackner, quoting from Thoroton, alludes to the 12th year of the reign of King Henry II, and also to the 15th year; "in both which years" the author writes, "Robert Fitz Ranulph was sheriff." [1]

It is intimated by one of these early writers (the later seemingly quoting from the earlier, and without show of evidence) that this High Sheriff, Lord Robert Fitz Randolph, was concerned with Lords Fitz-Urse, Tracy, Briton, and Morville, in the conspiracy which led to the death of Thomas à Becket. It is not charged that the High Sheriff actually participated in what these early writers called the "murther"; but they intimate that he filled the place which Saul filled at the stoning of Stephen — that he stood by and consented; and they say he afterward was obliged to pay certain religious penalties, or undergo certain penances, as a result of giving countenance to the death of à Becket.

The Fitz Randolphs were always intensely in earnest in whatever cause they espoused. The strain of controversy and antipathy between Henry II and Thomas a Becket was very intense and bitter. The nation was almost torn apart in the course of the great issue then made between kingly and constitutional rule on the one hand and prelatical control on the other.

At the basis of the character of the Scandinavian adventurers was a fearless aggressiveness. They were seldom content with the results of conquest, but were ever pressing on to further acquisitions. Humanitarianism in the broad sense, as we know and seek to cultivate it, was to them scarcely known. Mercy and kindness as personal duties were seldom in their thoughts; yet they were not devoid of a certain moral principle and aim, and they appeared to believe that the world was to be reformed through their conquest and dominion. With the acceptance of Christianity by the great Rolf, or Ralph, who became the first Duke of Normandy, a new element entered into the Norseman's mind and plan. It may not have included much of the gentleness and self-denial inculcated by the Nazarene, but it served to broaden the mind and enlarge the purpose of the fierce Norseman. It assisted also in the development of a respect for order and for law, even though the law was of the adventurers' own making. It thus came about, by the fusion of these widely different elements in character, that the leaders of the North, having the force and courage to conquer, had also the ability to administer upon what they had conquered.

In an excellent article on the Normans by E. A. Freeman, we read: "If the Norman was a born soldier, he was also a born lawyer. Randolf Flambard, working together the detached feudal usages of earlier times into a compact and logical system of feudal law, was as characteristic a type of the people as any warrior in the Conqueror's following. He was the organizer of an endless official army, of an elaborate technical system of administration, which had nothing like it in England before, but which grew up to perfection under Norman rulers. But nothing so well illustrates this formal side of the Norman character as the whole position of the Conqueror himself. His claim to the crown of England is something without earlier precedent, something as far as possible removed from the open violence of aggressors who have no pretexts with which to disguise their aggression. It rested on a mass of legal assumptions and subtleties, fallacious indeed, but ingenious, and, as the result proved, effective. His whole system of government, his confiscations, his grants, all that he did, was a logical deduction from one or two legal principles, arbitrary certainly in their conception, but strictly carried out to their results." [2]

Professor Freeman considers that this addiction to legal thought and process was chiefly inherited from the Scandinavian forefathers; but it seems quite as probable that this important influence which came in to qualify Norseman aggressiveness and lawlessness was due to the acceptance of such Christian principles as these brave and fierce men could grasp and appreciate.

Certain it is that in singular unity with the savage desires and purposes of power was a recognition of a Divine power and of the duty of worship. Professor Freeman says: "The Norman, a strict observer of forms in all matters, attended to the forms of religion with special care. No people were more bountiful to ecclesiastical bodies on both sides of the Channel; the foundation of a Benedictine monastery in the eleventh century, of a Cistercian monastery in the twelfth, seemed almost a matter of course on the part of a Norman baron. The Conqueror, beyond doubt, sincerely aimed at being a religious reformer, both in his duchy and in his kingdom. ...On the other hand, none were less inclined to submit to encroachments on the part of the ecclesiastical power, — the Conqueror himself least of all." [3]

These kinsmen and lieutenants of the Conqueror, whose families and lines of descent enter into the subject of this book, bore a generous part in the establishment and endowment of religious enterprises and institutions. The earlier of the Fitz Randolphs were amongst the knights of the Crusades. All the sons of Eudo and those who inherited from them were benefactors to the church and to the monasteries. St. Mary's Abbey at York, the Grey Friars at Richmond, and Jervaulx and Easby and Coverham Abbeys, and Thoralby and Spennithorne churches and many other institutions of like character, received large gifts at their hands.

The Abbey which was finally located at Coverham was originally founded at Swainby, Yorkshire, in 1190, by the wife of Robert Fitz Randolph, Lord of Middleham, and it was in that same year that he began the erection of the Castle at Middleham. In 1215 the establishment was transferred to Coverham, and there continued until the Dissolution by Henry VIII, though it is said to have been meanwhile subject from time to time to Scottish depredations and injuries.

At Coverham we find several effigies in stone of an interesting character. The author of "Romantic Richmondshire" writes of them as follows: "They are of the surcoat period, sculptured in crusading panoply of the time of Henry III to Edward II. They are much mutilated, but are worthy of the best care — two of them being probably the oldest sculptures of their kind extant in Yorkshire. There can, I think, be little doubt that one represents the powerful Ranulph Fitz Robert, who translated the monks of Swainby to Coverham in 1215. He was great-grandnephew of the Conqueror's kinsman Earl Alan, first Lord of Richmondshire after the Conquest, and died in 1215. He was interred with great pomp in the Chapter House at Coverham along with his mother, whose remains had been brought hither from Swainby, where they had lain since her death in

1195. Another effigy (a mere torso— a ruthless destruction due perhaps to the Scottish raid on Coverham after Bannockburn in 1314) may represent his son, Ralph Fitz Ranulph, founder, or co-founder, of the monastery of the Grey Friars at Richmond, who died in 1270, and whose heart was buried in the church of the Grey Friars and his bones at Coverham."

Effigies, Coverham Abbey

Whellan's "History and Topography" sums up this record, and the conjecture concerning these effigies, as follows: "In the reign of Edward, the Confessor, Middleham was a manor belonging to Ghilpatric, a Dane. The Norman Conquest left it a waste, and in that condition it was when Allen, Earl of Brittany, who had a grant of Richmondshire from the Conqueror, gave it to his brother Ribald. This Ribald, the first Norman Lord of Middleham, gave to God and St. Mary at York, and the Abbot Gosfrid, in perpetual alms for the soul of Beatrix, his wife (daughter of Ivo de Tallabois by the Countess Lucy of Lincoln, the sister of Earl Morcar), and that of Earl Allen [Alan] five carucates [4] of land in Burniston; and after the death of his wife he became a monk in the said Abbey of St. Mary. By his wife, Beatrix, he had a son Ralph, surnamed Faylbois; to him. Earl Stephen, his uncle (Lord of the honour of Richmond), by his Charter and the delivery of a Danish hatchet, confirmed Middleham, and all the lands which Ribald, his father, possessed at the time he became a monk. By his wife, Agatha, daughter of Robert de Brus of Skelton, he had a son, Robert, surnamed Fitz-Ranulph or Fitz Randolph, to whom Conan, Earl of Richmond, gave the forest of Wensleydale, with common pasture. This Robert, in 1190, commenced the erection of the Castle of Middleham. After his death, his widow, Helewisa, daughter of the famous justiciary of Henry II, Ralph de Glanville, [5] by authority of a bull granted by Pope Clement II, founded a monastery of white canons at Swainby, near Pickhall. She died in 1195, and was buried at Swainby. Her son, Rahulph Fitz Robert, or Ranulpus, Lord of Middleham, translated the monks of Swainby to Coverham, near Middleham, in 1214, and conferred on them the Church of Coverham and many lands and tenements. He also had the bones of his mother brought from Swainby and buried in the chapter house at Coverham. He died in 1251, and was buried at Coverham; and the more rigid of the effigies, still preserved there, is supposed to represent him.

Ralph Fitz Randolph, his son, was the founder, or one of the founders, of the Friars Minor at Richmond.

A rich and elegant figure at Coverham is conjectured to belong to him. By his wife, Anastasia, daughter of William, Lord Percy, he had a daughter and heiress, Maria, called "Mary of Middleham," who married Robert de Neville, Lord of Raby (lineally descended in the paternal line from Uchtred, the great Saxon Earl of Northumberland), but the union was of short duration. This lady is said to have been fair and gentle, founded a chantry at Thoraldby, in 1316, for her own soul and those of her father and mother, and of Sir Robert de Neville, formerly her husband, and all their ancestors and heirs. She remained a widow nearly fifty years, dwelling on her own inheritance, and, dying in 1320, was buried in the choir at Coverham beside her husband."

This whole region of Yorkshire, or, as this part of it is sometimes called, Richmondshire, is replete with associations of fascinating interest. Here was produced the family that gave birth to the famous poet and Biblical scholar. Miles Coverdale; [6] the father of William Makepeace Thackeray was here trained for his life work, and it might almost be said that the foot-falls of George Fox and of John Wesley are still heard over the Yorkshire hills. In choosing one other name out of the many worthy of mention, I take the name most dear to American hearts — that of Washington.

Coverham Abbey

"The village of Yorkshire now called Whashton, anciently spelt Whassyngton and also called Washington-Juxta-Ravensworth, has the distinction [says Speight] of having given name to the family which in the eighteenth century produced the celebrated General George Washington, First President of the United States of America, who was descended from Leonard Washington of Warton, county of Lancaster...whose son Laurence emigrated to America in 1659 and settled in Virginia. Leonard's ancestor was Robert Washington, Lord of Milbourne, county of Westmoreland, of the time of Henry III, whose descent is traced by Harrison to Bonde, Lord of Washington-Juxta-Ravensworth, to whom his father, Akary fil Bardulf, Lord of Ravensworth, gave the manor of Washington in the time of King Stephen." [7]

Two facts of some interest here appear: one is that Robert Washington, Lord of Milbourne, Westmoreland, and Henry Fitz Randolph, Lord of Ravensworth, were cotemporaries of the period of Henry III; the other fact is that they were both descended from one member (Bardolf) of the already mentioned band of brothers, sons of Eudo, connections of William the Conqueror; and to him reference has already been made as the ancestor of Lord Henry Fitz Randolph; and it also appears that in the thirteenth and fourteenth centuries Henry Fitz Randolph and his descendants held the same lordship of Ravensworth, which had been held in the twelfth century by his progenitor who was also the progenitor of Washington, namely, Akary, the son of Bardulf — or Bardulph, or Bardolf.

[1] Referring to Blackner's History of Nottingham, Appendix, page 448, we find that the author quotes from Dr. Thoroton's historical description of the Forest of Shirewood, as follows: "When this forest of Shirewood was first made, I find not; the first mention of it I do find is in Henry the Second's time, but I conceive it a forest before, for William Peverell in the first year of Henry the Second (which is mistaken for the fifth year of King Stephen) doth answer *de Placitis Forestae* in this county. It seems he had the whole profit and command of this forest for his estate, which after coming to the crown, the sheriff (8. H. 2.) in the account of his farm prays to be discharged of £4 *in vasto Forestal;* and in the tenth year of the same king's reign he prays the like discharge of £4 for the waste, as also allowance of £6 6s. paid to the constable, eight foresters, and a warrener, and to the cannons of Shirewood for alms £40, which I conceive to be the prior and monks of Newstede, then newly founded by Henry II. In the next year the sheriff of the county, Randulphus filius Engalrami, answers *de censu Forestae;* and in the twelfth year, Robert de Catz, Lord of Laxton, a fermor, answers for it. £20, and (15. H. 2.) Reginaldus de Lud answers the like sum of £20 pro censu Forestae, in both which years Robert Fitz Ranulph was sheriff."

[2] In the able and scholarly work written by Henry Offley Wakeman, M.A., Fellow of All Souls' College, Oxford, entitled "The History of the Church of England from the Earliest Times," at page 77, the author says, in writing of the period of Edward the Confessor, "No wonder that the eyes of Edward were dazzled by the brilliancy of the Norman race. Ever since the days when Rolf the Northman had won his duchy of Normandy by the sword in 912, and secured it by his acceptance of Christianity, the Normans had played no small part in the world. Rapidly assimilating French speech and French civilization, infusing French quickness and vivacity into the deep but impetuous current of the Northern character, bringing the fervid and imaginative religious spirit

of Scandinavia under the orderly spirits of the Western church, the Normans claimed the leadership of the world in the eleventh century because they were best fitted to lead it."

[3] Hume considers that the lowest depression of human ignorance and degradation between the culmination of Roman civilization on the one hand and the revival of learning, which accompanied the introduction of the art of printing on .the other, was the point at which William the Norman began his wonderful career. On page 372 of the first volume of his history he writes "The period in which the people of Christendom were the lowest sunk in ignorance, and consequently in disorders of every kind, may justly be fixed at the eleventh: century, about the age of William the Conqueror, and from that era the sun of science, beginning to reascend, threw out many gleams of lights which preceded the full morning when letters were revived in the fifteenth century."

[4] About five hundred acres.

[5] The blood of the great de Glanville in the entire line of Fitz Randolphs, from the sons of Robert Fitz Randolph, Lord of Middleham, and for fully seven centuries elapsing since this union, is deserving of more than a passing notice. As d soldier, a jurist and a leader of men of mind and power, he possessed exceptionally high qualities. It was he, for example, who took prisoner the Scotch King William the Lion, at Alnwick in 1174, and thus for the first time Scotland and the Scottish church was brought under subjection to England. Encyc. Brit. XXI, 484.

[6] Miles Coverdale was almoner to Queen Catherine Parr. Margaret Neville was a maid of honour at the marriage of her stepmother, Catherine Parr, to Henry VIII in 1543.

Speaking of Wensleydale alone (in which is the Castle of Middleham) the Catholic historian Barker says "It is no mean boast for so secluded a valley to have produced a Queen of England, a Prince of Wales, a Cardinal Bishop, three other Archbishops, five Bishops, three Chancellors and two Chief Justices of England; not to mention the distinguished Abbots, Earls, Barons and Knights who were also natives."

[7] Gale brings forward the crude land-record, of the time of King Henry III, thus "Quassyngton: Sunt ibi 4 caruc. terrae, quarum Ranulphus filius Henrici tenet 2 & Rogerus tenet alias 2 de Hugone filio Henrici, and Hugo de Comite. & Comes de Rege."

"Canic" is abbreviation for *carucate* — as much land as could be cultivated by one plow, usually a hundred acres: thus "4 caruc." = 400 acres approximately. The quantity varied according to soil and husbandry.

Chapter Five - Middleham Castle and Some of its Occupants

The localities just named (namely, the home of the Fitz Randolphs, descended from Bardulf, and the birthplace of the reformer, Wycliffe) are within an easy morning walk of Middleham in Yorkshire, where still stands the magnificent ruin of the castle built more than seven centuries ago by Lord Robert Fitz Randolph, the grandson of Ribald, who was the brother of Bardulf and of Alan.

This castle was built somewhat later than the reign of King Stephen (whose mother, Adela, was a daughter of William the Conqueror, as was also Constantia the wife of Alan); [1] but the rage for building castles by the nobility was well under way during King Stephen's reign. In order to conciliate the barons who remained true to him in his numerous and desperate quarrels with various parties and powers, Stephen allowed them to build castles —each of which became a center of power, and sometimes of tyranny. Hundreds of castles were built during his reign and the reigns of the earliest Henrys. Many of these have practically disappeared. A few have in later days been converted into baronial residences, and many more fell into ruin in the course of feudal wars and of the consolidation of kingly power. Still others were rendered untenable during the brief but strenuous period of the Cromwelliad. To this last destructive potency is attributed the present condition of Middleham Castle, though the circumstances attending its partial demolition are but vaguely known. The Castle was, however, of such huge bulk and immense original strength and stoutness as to resist all efforts to destroy it utterly. It is, therefore, still, now, even in its existing condition of ruin, one of the most prominent and most interesting exemplifications of mediaeval castle-building.

"As a specimen of Architecture, Middleham Castle is a unique but not a happy work," says Whitaker. "The Norman keep, the fortress of the first Lords, not being sufficient for the vast trains and princely habits of the Nevilles, was enclosed, at no long period before Leland's time, by a complete quadrangle, which almost entirely darkened what was dark enough before; and the first structure now stands completely isolated in the center of a later work of no very ample dimensions within, and nearly as high as itself, I must, however, suppose that the original keep was surrounded by a bailey occupying nearly the space of the present quadrangular work.

"Within the original building are the remains of a magnificent hall and chapel; but it might be difficult to pronounce whether the first or the second work consists of the more massive and indissoluble grout-work.

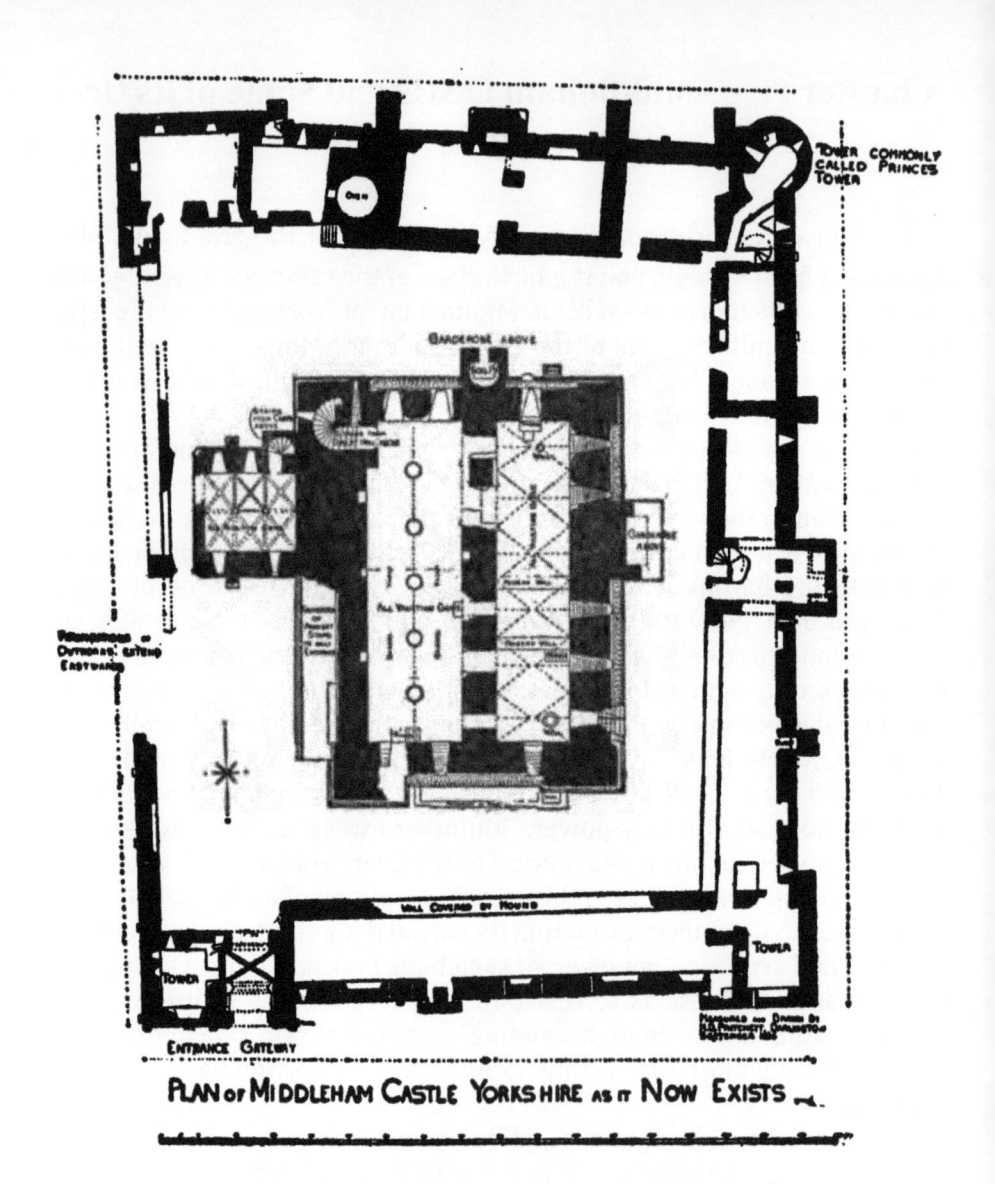

"The ruins of this once magnificent castle are extensive and interesting. The best view of them is from the southwest. Most of the walls are still of great height. The large gateway on the north side is quite perfect, and consists of a circular arch constructed under a pointed one, similar to those of the gateway of Easby Abbey.

"The chapel may be distinctly traced; but broken fragments of the walls and rubbish have accumulated from the height of from six to ten feet above the original floors, A few years ago, a portion of the moat remained on the south side of the castle."

The Castle

Various writers have held it as strongly probable that William the Conqueror from time to time visited Middleham. Such visits, however, must have been made more than a century prior to the commencement of the castle by Robert Fitz Randolph. It is also said that Ribald, the grandfather of Robert the Castle-builder, spent much time here and hereabouts. He certainly was Lord of Middleham. It remained, however, for a later age and for those who followed these notable personages to render most famous this center of ducal power and ambition.

A little more than fifty years ago, Mr. W. G. M. Jones Barker, a writer of merit, and a devout Catholic, wrote a History of Wensleydale, in which he summarizes thus a part of the history we are considering:

"William had bestowed the domains of murdered Edwin, Saxon Earl of Mercia, of which Wensleydale formed part, on his follower and relative Alan Rufus, First Earl of Richmond, who shortly after began to build the castle at that place. Alan gave the manor of Middleham to his brother Ribald [2] who, probably, resided there; and he, after the death of his wife, Beatrix, became a monk of St. Mary's at York. He appears to have been liberal to the church. To his grandson, Robert, Conan, Earl of Richmond, granted the Forest of Wensleydale with common pasture; and this Robert, in 1190, began the Castle of Middleham. The family in likelihood previously resided in Ghilpatric Fortress."

It will be understood that this Fortress of Ghilpatric was on an eminence just above the site chosen for the Castle of Middleham.

The Keep

King Richard III, himself a descendant of Robert Fitz Randolph, married his cousin Anne (also a descendant of the same great baron), and occupied the castle at Middleham; and his only son, Edward, was born there in 1473 and died there in 1484. Barker says: — "Richard III possessed Middleham Castle, and that fortress was held by him when he fell at Bosworth Field, August 22, 1485. It passed with Richard's other possessions to Henry VII."

Speight says: "The fiery Duke of Gloucester, afterwards Richard III, [3] having married Warwick's daughter, the Lady Anne Neville, whom his falchion had made a widow, [4] was glad to escape from Pontefract to the 'home of his domestic affections' at Middleham, which had been the inheritance of his wife. He was probably sojourning at the castle when the news reached him of the death of his brother, Edward IV, in April, 1483. On the 6th of July following he was crowned at Westminster. It was in an apartment since called the 'Prince's Chamber,' in the round tower at the southwest angle of the castle at Middleham, that Edward, Prince of Wales, the much-loved son of Richard III, was born. Tradition says that the little lad, in whom his father had centered all his fondest hopes, met with an inexplicably suspicious death at Middleham in the spring of 1484. His father and mother were then staying at Nottingham, and when the sad news was conveyed to them, it is said they gave way to the wildest fits of despair. The king would not be comforted, and the queen-mother completely broke down under the sudden and crushing sorrow. They lost no time in repairing to Middleham to gaze on the 'cold, dear face of their only loved son, at sight of which, old Croydon,' the historian, tells us, 'you might have seen the father and mother in a state bordering on madness.' The mother never recovered, and died, it is said, of grief, within twelve months of her son, at the early age of thirty-one."

Barker quotes the following details from an older writer — Leland: "Middleham Castel joyneth harde to the town side, and is the fairest castel of Richmondshire, next Bolton, and the castel hath a parke by it, called Sonske, and another caulied West Parke, and Gaunless (Wanlass) be well woddid. Middleham is a praty market toune, and standeth on a rokky hill, on the top whereof is the castel, meatly well diked."

"All the utter parte of the castelle was of the very new setting of the Lord Nevile, called Darabi; [5] the inner part of Middleham Castel was of the ancient building of the Fitz Randolph."

"There be four or five parks about Middleham, and longing to it, whereof some be reasonably woodyed." [6]

Meantime, between the days of Robert Fitz Randolph and the accession to the crown of his descendant Richard III, Middleham Castle saw much of the stir of feudal life and conflict. Of some part of this, the story is told in Bulwer Lytton's novel, "The Last of the Barons." A central point of interest in this fascinating novel is the Fitz Randolph Castle, a home of the Earl of Warwick, whom the novelist calls "The Last of the Barons."

The author of "Romantic Richmondshire," again writing of this castle, says: "The Keep is the oldest portion of the building and was of the foundation of Fitz Randolphs about the end of the twelfth century. The exterior parts of the castle are fourteenth-century work built by the Nevilles — the whole forming a grand parallelogram 210 feet by 180 feet, flanked by a tower at each angle. It was encompassed by a broad and deep moat fed by natural springs, and portions of this remained tolerably perfect up to about 1830, when the space was filled up. The gateway of the castle on the north side is almost perfect. The large banqueting hall and the chapel also remain interesting features. The tenacity of the mortar is something to remark upon."

It was in this castle that the great Earl of Warwick (descended from the Fitz Randolphs of Middleham and grandson of Ralph, or Randolph, first Earl of Westmoreland), known as "The King-maker," held high carnival and fed an army of fighting retainers. Of him and his entertainments here, as well as in London, Barker quotes from an old authority: — "Six oxen were eaten at a breakfast and every tavern was filled of his meet, for he that had any acquaintance in that house, he should have as much sodden and roast as he might carry upon a long dagger." [7]

Such was the lavish hospitality of the Lords of Middleham of five hundred years ago. In those days of the historic Earl of Warwick ("the last of the feudal barons, a master in camp and in court, the setter-up and plucker-down of kings") the Court of England, as Bulwer Lytton pertinently observes, was not Windsor, nor Shene, nor Westminster, nor the Tower, but it was Middleham in Yorkshire.

The Fitz-Randolph Castle at Middleham was then the home and place of assemblage of mighty men and of dames of England's choicest beauty and of the flower of all her gallantry.

Church of St. Mary and St. Akelda
Endowed by the Earlier Fitz Randolphs and by Certain of Their Royal Descendents

Summing up a few particulars, we note here (at the risk of some repetition) that it was Mary Fitz Randolph Neville's great, great, great grandson (son of Ralph, or Randolph, First Earl of Westmoreland, and of his second wife, Joan Beaufort) who was Earl of Salisbury; and Salisbury's son by his wife, the heiress of Thomas de Montacute, [8] was Warwick, 'The Kingmaker." When Warwick died, the castle passed to Richard III, who, as has been seen, had married Warwick's daughter Anne. After Henry VII defeated Richard at the battle of Bosworth, Middleham reverted to the Tudor Crown. In 1647, during the time of the Commonwealth, it was dismantled. About the time of the Restoration of Charles II, it was sold to the City of London by the Crown. In 1662, Edward Wood, Esq., bought the castle, and in 1670 he came into possession of the entire manor. In 1889, the whole property was purchased by Samuel Cunliffe Lister, Esq., at a cost, as I am informed, of £50,000. On Mr. Lister was subsequently conferred the title of "Lord Masham," and *about this time* he gave utterance to a clever *mot* in a speech at a meeting of the Antiquarian Society. "For the second time in its history," said he, "the noble Castle of Middleham is in possession of The *Last* of the Barons." His son, the later Lord Masham [pronounced Mas-ham, or Ma*ss*am] has shown considerate care to the venerable pile, supporting and protecting the old walls wherever necessary, and placing an honest and intelligent care-taker in charge.

Mr. W. G. M. J. Barker, in his "Three Days in Wensleydale," referring to the ruins of this fortress, says, "Altogether the castle, by historic recollections, is rendered one of the most interesting in the north of England. As we pace its deserted courts, or stand within its roofless walls, imagination may well recall the bygone. The trumpet sounds — the armor clashes. The gorgeous Edward [9] — the munificent Richard — fair Anne of Warwick — her duchess sister, Isabella of Clarence — and their stately sire — people these desolate rooms. Lady, Knight, Demoiselle and Demoiseau flit past us — brilliant pageantry! Anon the scene changes. Night hovers over the castle. The young moon vainly struggles with the dim clouds —torches supply her place. There are guards and a prisoner — we hear the death-axe fall on the unhappy Falconbridge. We start from our day-dream — all are gone — feasters and sufferers, nobles and soldiers. We are standing in a banquet hall deserted, and the jackdaw's crow awakens the echoes instead of the trumpet's sound!" Dr. Whitaker says, "As it is, majestic in decay. Middleham Castle is, as an object, the noblest work of man in the county of Richmondshire. The views up and down Wensleydale from the windows of this castle are delightful and picturesque."

The writer is tempted at this point to break in upon his own narrative and to venture to apologize for one who has perhaps in the course of history had too few apologists, and who appears to have been unconscionably maligned. King Richard III, of England, was an ambitious man who lived in a cruel age. When he died bravely on Bosworth field his own particular line of princes failed. No one was left to speak for him, and his victorious enemy, Henry, Duke of Richmond, who became Henry VII, established a new dynasty, that of the Tudors, one of whose objects was to asperse and destroy the character of his predecessor and opponent. Friends of Richard were speedily cowed and silenced. By the Tudor historians and dramatists, Richard was represented as a hump-backed monster. He never was this. Doubtless he was supremely and fiercely bent on accomplishing his ends; but he was not more vindictive or cruel than other princes. He forgave and restored Stanley, and Stanley ungratefully turned against him at the last moment in the decisive battle in which Richard fell. [10]

Royal Gallery Portrait of Richard III of England

The smothering of his brother's sons in the tower was never proved against Richard — though he may have been responsible for this crime. He was courageous, enterprising and energetic, and was an earnest patron of learning in a day when learning had not yet become popular, and when princes feared it. Even Bulwer, who follows Hume in denouncing this king, is compelled to own that Richard was a protector and promoter of learning. [11] He was also, according to his day and light, a patron of religion. The seal of the church at Middleham (a copy of which lies before the writer as readopted in Richard's honor by the chapter, or deanery, so late as the year 1742) shows that he established and patronized it as a Collegiate Church. Barker says that the king's purpose to rebuild the church edifice at Middleham was frustrated by his death. He loved this church as he loved his wife and his son and his castle at Middleham and his Yorkshiremen; and these Yorkshiremen believed in him absolutely — believed in his bravery, in his truth, and in his right and ability to govern, and were ever ready to follow him through any peril. Prothero says in effect that the story of Richard's deformity was derived from his enemies' malignity and from a misunderstanding of his name "Crouchback"; and that, but for certain other qualities, his courage, energy and ability would have made him a great and honored name.

Bulwer pays a certain tribute to Richard's morality and steadfastness, and to his peculiar and mysterious power, in the scene which he describes as taking place in Middleham Castle, in which he imagines the great Earl of Warwick in the course of conversation with his brother, the Archbishop, and as saying — whilst they stood looking at Richard conversing with the younger daughter of the mighty Earl — "He has his father's face; but yet the boy is to me a riddle. That he will be bold in battle and wise in council I foresee; but would he had more of a young man's follies! There is a medium between Edward's wantonness and Richard's sanctimony; and he who in the heyday of youth's blood scowls alike upon sparkling wine and smiling woman may hide in his heart darker and more sinful fancies. But fie on me! I will not wrongfully mistrust his father's son!"

The Royal Gallery portrait of Richard is far from being a representation of a brutish character. It is the portrait of a gentleman — of a character something like that of the sensitive and thoughtful Hamlet of Shakespeare's play. Richard's life and example may not be on the whole one worthy of commendation to posterity, but he need not (to use a mediaeval word) be held up as a "scarebabe"; and history should be fair even when written under such inspiration as that of Henry VII, whose misdemeanors and meannesses and cruelties far outnumbered those of any son of Cicely, the Rose of Raby.

Lack of space forbids dwelling upon the interesting old church of St. Akelda, at Middleham, in which the apparently severe and cruel Richard HI was so deeply interested, and in whose parish-house in later days the beloved Canon Kingsley lived and wrote. It was endowed with glebe lands by Ralph Neville, great-grandson of Robert Fitz Randolph, Lord of Middleham. We have seen that Richard III constituted Middleham Church a collegiate church, and granted lands to endow it; but on his defeat and death at the battle of Bosworth, Henry VII seized the church lands as well as the castle; so, having nothing to lose at the time of the Reformation, the honorary Constitution was left untouched, and the clergy were called dean and sub-dean, and had so recently the power to confer honorary canonries that Charles Kingsley derived his first title of canon from this church; and in his published life some beautiful letters are given, written by him from Middleham when he went to receive the dignity of canon.

[1] Some historians say of Alan Rufus, first Earl of Richmond: - others say of Alan Fergant, son of Hoel. Gale holds to the latter opinion.

[2] The entry in the Conqueror's book of "Domesday," compiled by Randolph Flambard, is as follows: "In Medelai ad Geld. 5 Caruc. & 8 Caruc. possunt esse. Ibi habuit Ghilpatrik Manerium: nunc habet Ribald & vasturn est" Medelai was the name given to Middleham by the Romans. It was a central point, or crossways of importance, in the days of the Roman occupation of Britain.

[3] See Halsted's Richard III, Vol. I, page 298; Shakespeare's King Richard III.

[4] Her sister Isabel was the wife of George, Duke of Clarence, brother of Edward IV and Richard III. Anne's first husband was Edward, Prince of Wales, son of Henry VI. He was slain at the battle of Tewkesbury in 1471.

[5] The antiquarian Stowe calls Ralph Neville (the great Earl of Westmoreland) "Dan Raby Nevel." Hollinshed calls him "Dauraby." Leland (as above) calls him Darabi. "Dan" (still farther abbreviated to "Dn") was the common rendering of Dominus (Lord) equivalent to the Spanish Don. Longstaffe in his work entitled "Richmondshire, its ancient Lords and Edifices" suggests that "Daw" may have been "the diminutive of Ralph or Randolph.

[6] It is hard at first to believe that the antiquary John Leland, or Leyland, or Laylonde (for, like some of the Fitz Randolphs, he appears to have kept on hand a choice assortment of names of his own family) wrote the best English of the time of Henry VIII. He was a scholar and linguist, having been educated at Oxford under the famous grammarian Lily and having travelled much on the continent as well as in England. Even Queen Elizabeth spoke better Latin than English; and whilst Oliver Cromwell's acts were prompt and well-aimed, his English words were involved and slow. Can we wonder — knowing this — that if today one wishes to read land deeds of the fourteenth to the sixteenth centuries in England he must pore over Norman-French documents; and if one aspires to be historian or genealogist and learn of the deeds of men or their descent, he must translate records kept by the English fathers in Latin.

[7] Some of Warwick's close kinship displayed equally great liberality and extravagance. The details of the Installation Feast of George Neville (Warwick's brother) as Archbishop of York are given by Froude. These festal provisions include eighty oxen, six wild bulls, a thousand sheep, three hundred hogs and as many calves, four hundred head of venison, three thousand geese, twenty-three hundred capons, vast flocks of peacocks, pigeons, cranes, partridges, pheasants, woodcocks, plovers, curlews and quails, with custards, tarts and pasties *ad lib.,* and of ale three hundred tuns and of wine one hundred and four tuns. — Froude Hist. of Eng., Vol. I, page 52.

[8] Through whom the Salisbury title and wealth descended.

[9] Edward IV was entertained at the Castle of Middleham by his cousin the brave Earl of Warwick. It is also generally believed that at one time Warwick held this king as a prisoner in the castle. Stowe asserts this and Shakespeare writes on similar lines in Henry VI, Third part. Act 4. So accomplished a historical scholar as G. W. Prothero, M.A., Fellow of Kings College, Cambridge, writes. "Edward, whose troops were defeated at Edgecote, fell into War-

wick's hands and was removed to his castle at Middleham," *Vide Encycl. Brit.,* XXIV, 882. Warwick's strenuous life was largely given to making and unmaking — by turns — Edward IV and Henry VI. Finally he went to his own undoing at the battle of Barnet on Easter Day, 1471. Bulwer describes young Richard's participation in that fight. A dozen years later this young Richard was king and himself in possession of the castle.

[10] Retribution was not slow in falling upon Stanley. After he had placed on the head of the first Tudor king the crown of Richard III, which he claimed to find on Bosworth field, he was accused by Clifford of disloyalty. It was shown that he had made an indiscreet remark favorable to the pretender Perkin Warbeck. It was slender basis for action on Henry's part, but Stanley was rich and Henry was avaricious. Off went Stanley's head and into Henry's coffers went Stanley's wealth. — Hume II, 422.

[11] Bulwer writes in his "Last of the Barons," — referring to the "invention" of printing, just coming into use in the latter part of the fifteenth century — "Richard III during his brief reign spared no pains to circulate to the utmost the invention." Goldwin Smith says of Richard — "By a statute freely admitting books he marked the age and did credit to himself."— Political Hist, Vol. I, p. 274.

Chapter Six - From Yorkshire to Nottinghamshire and Back, with a Short Study in Heraldry

We have in the course of this book considered especially *three* prominent characters of the Fitz Randolph name, men who sprung from the same original Norman stock: and any one of whom might have seemed to be the leading ancestor of the Fitz Randolphs of Nottinghamshire and of the United States. It may safely be added in view of the relative rarity of this Norman name, and of all facts and circumstances to be considered, that the line of descent *could hardly have been outside of these three;* and from this it would follow that upon the clear elimination of two of these, the line of descent must have been from the one remaining source. The first is Robert Fitz Randolph, Lord of Middleham; the second is Robert Fitz Randolph, High Sheriff of Nottingham and Derby, and close friend of Henry II; and the third is Henry Fitz Randolph, Lord of Ravensworth. As to the second (Robert, the High Sheriff), we are repeatedly informed that his male line, proceeding with his son, William, ceased with his grandson, Thomas, the last Baron of Norton, who died without issue, leaving his inheritance to his sisters. This is so stated in Nicholas' "Historic Peerage of England" and is re-asserted by Banks, Baxter and other authors, and remains uncontradicted. As to the third mentioned, the noble Lord of Ravensworth, we find that his lineage, chiefly if not exclusively, took the name of Fitz Hugh, with a coat-of-arms practically identical with that which the High Sheriff bore, and somewhat similar to that of the Fitz Randolphs of Middleham, but still distinctly separate from the latter; [1] and to this last fact we shall again refer. All these lived either in the time of the second or of the third King Henry. As to the first of this noble trio, Robert Fitz Randolph, Lord of Middleham, we have shown positively that his blood descended in the posterity of his third son through the thirteenth, fourteenth and fifteenth centuries in the line of the Fitz Randolphs of Spennithorne, whose home was just beyond the river Ure, or Yore, [2] in sight of the original Fitz Randolph Castle at Middleham. Of this Spennithorne family the last father of a family of the name at that place was Ralph (or Randolph) Fitz Randolph, who lived in the latter half of the sixteenth century in the time of Edward VI, and whose daughter, Agnes, married Marmaduke Wyvill, Esquire, ancestor of a line of brave, loyal and distinguished men. But, a little earlier than this, at least one of the tribe of Fitz Randolphs had appeared, and had come into some prominence about a hundred miles south from Spennithorne in the northwest portion of Nottinghamshire. I refer especially to Christopher Fitz Randolph, who was a subject of Henry VIII, father of Edward VI. Thoroton in his "Antiquities of Nottinghamshire" (published in 1677), refers to the marriage of a certain Christopher Fitz Randolph with Joan or Joane, daughter of Cuthbert Langton, of Langton Hall. The same Cuthbert Langton (according to the same authority) "enfeoffed" certain lands in Huknall Torkard (Nottinghamshire) and other lands in the same shire, and in other shires, to half a dozen personages and persons, amongst whom was a John Fitz Randolph. It thus appears that in the Tudor day certain of the name of Fitz Randolph held property and position in Nottinghamshire.

In the appendix of John Blackner's History of Nottingham (already briefly quoted from) we read of "A perambulation of the forest of Sheerewood made the nineth day of September in the Thirtyeth year of the Reigne of King Henry the Eighth (by the grace of God of England and ffrance King, defender of the faith. Lord of Ireland, and Supreme head upon earth of the English Church); by Robert Brymesley; Gabriel Berwicke, Richard Perepoint, Esq., Alexander Mening, Christopher Fitzrandole, Robert Whitemore, John Walker, Maurite Orrell, John Garnon, John Palmer. Gentlemen: Robert Levett, William Mellars, Robert Rawson, John Losscowe, John Bristow and Robert North, Regarders of the said forest of Sheerewood, which perambulation begun at the Kings Castle of Nottingham."

We turn now with more particularity to the heraldic arms of the Fitz Randolphs in confirmation of the conclusion that the Fitz Randolphs of Nottinghamshire of the fifteenth and sixteenth centuries (with whom Edward Fitz Randolph of Langton Hall, and also of Massachusetts and

New Jersey, forms the link connecting our family of to-day with more ancient days) were descended from the Lords of Middleham of the twelfth and thirteenth centuries, and thus from the near kinship of William the Conqueror.

In "Burke's General Armory," at page 357, we find the arms of a certain Fitz Ranulph of the time of Henry II stated thus — "Az. two chev. or." In the same connection the Fitz Randolph arms (Co. Northumberland) is given as "or, a chief, indented, az." In the Appendix of Robson's British Herald, Vol. III, we have the arms of the Fitz Randolphs of Spennithome given thus, "Az, a chief, indented, or." and to this, as borne out in the several examples now to be seen at St. Michael's Church of Spennithome, we shall refer a little later on.

Robson's British Herald, Vol. I, gives the following: "Fitz Ranulph (Derby & Notts. Temp. Henry II) Az: two chev. or." [This applied to Robert, High Sheriff, close friend to Henry II.]

"Fitz Randall, az. a chief indented, or."

"Fitz Randolfe, az. fretty or, a chief of the last."

"Fitz Randolph [N. Umb.] or, a chief, indented, az." [3]

Now, Burke's General Armory gives (from a Nottingham visitation of 1614) the arms of Edward Fitz Randolph, and of the Langton Hall Fitz Randolfs, as "Ar. a chief, indented, az." And Burke gives, for the same, *a crest* — "On a chapeau, or, turned up, az, a wyvern of the last."

Of course, it is understood that "or" stands for gold, or for yellow; "ar" for argent, silver, or white; and "az" for azure, or blue.

**ARMS OF THE
FITZ RANDOLPHS**

**FITZ-RANDOLPH
Lord of Middleham
A. D. 1190.**

From Armorial Shields of Early and Important Families of Northern England, as Given by W. G. M. Jones Barker,, in the Second Edition of His Work, Published in London in 1856, Entitled Historical and Topographical Account of Wensleydale and the Valley of the Yore.

Here, then (irrespective of the arms of the High Sheriff and of the Lord of Ravensworth), we find scarcely any change in the family escutcheon from the day of Robert the Castle-builder during a period of about four hundred and fifty years (say 1164 to 1614). Indeed, taking the whole record together, it may fairly be said that during that period this line of family and descent had practically the same heraldic device and blazonry — this particular coat-of-arms remaining in the Fitz Randolph line without notable alteration through the rule of the feudal Norman dukes, through the Plantagenet, York and Lancaster regimes, and continuing thus from before the founding of Middleham Castle in the twelfth century down to the Tudor days in which lived Christopher of Nottinghamshire and his son Edward, "forebears" of the Pilgrim Edward. It antedates the Spennithorne Fitz Randolphs (who, as we have seen, were in a straight line descended from Robert of Middleham), and was borne also by them; and after their day the same form, with scarcely a variation even as to color arrangement, continued to be borne by Christopher and Edward, ancestors of our New Jersey family. We could hardly look for stronger proof of source of lineage, for it must be kept in mind that, as time went on, these heraldic symbols were most jealously guarded by English families, and most strictly watched and regulated by royal authority, inquisition and "visitation." [4]

Ulshaw Bridge, R. Ure.

For the Building of a bridge at this point, near Middleham, Randolph, Lord of Middleham, and first Earl of Westmoreland, Made Provision in His Will, Dated October 18, 1424. [Vide Latin Record in Honoris de Richmond: Observationes, p. 245.]

So, whilst it is not doubted that the Spennithorne *properties* of Ralph Fitz Randolph descended (in the later Tudor days) to the honorable family of Wyville through the marriage of Ralph's daughter Agnes, it appears entirely possible that in a somewhat earlier generation some junior member or members of this Spennithorne family might have gone a little way off into Nottinghamshire. The blood of the family had commingled with princes, but the Spennithorne branch had been quiet, loyal and unpretending for centuries, enjoying the name and fame of their house and a comfortable inheritance, but without important titles to contend for or insist upon. [5] So the property descended regularly to the eldest son, and finally to a daughter. The mind bent on genealogical research pauses here to weigh a possibility that a male member of the family, probably in a position of juniority, may have broken away from Spennithorne and gone a little way southward to father a family who should develop a hunger for broader opportunities and in a newer world. But before accepting such a hypothesis — however reasonable — let us make further exploration.

Before quite turning away from Yorkshire to follow the progress of the Fitz Randolphs in Nottinghamshire, let us pause a little longer amongst the baronial residences, churches and forests of lovely Wensleydale. Not far from Middleham, nor from Richmond, was the hamlet, or township, of Bainbridge, spelt "Beyntbrigge" in the ancient chronicles. The luxury of litigation in which we moderns generously (and generally) indulge was not unknown to our forefathers. In 1228 the Earl of Chester and Lincoln claimed certain ownership and control in Wensleydale, and summoned Randolph, son of Robert Fitz Randolph, Lord of Middleham, to answer "by what warrant he made towns and raised edifices in the Earl's forest of Wensleydale." The answer was "The town of Beyntbrigge was of the ancestors of the said Ranulph by the service of keeping that forest, so that they should have there abiding twelve foresters with a horse for each." This condition of care and control continued through successive generations.

Mr. Barker in his "Historical and Topographical Account of Wensleydale" refers to this, quoting copiously from ancient Latin records and historical notes. He makes mention of Ranulph de Glanville, who was Lord Justiciary of England from 1181 to 1185, and was also Lord of Coverham, and was father-in-law of Robert Fitz Randolph, Lord of Middleham; and the historian tells us that, after his death, "William, son of Gamell, had ward of the forest till the death of the Lady Helewisa of Middleham, whose husband predeceased her. Afterwards Hubert Walter, Archbishop of Canterbury (1193-1207), Chief Justice of England (1194-1196), and Chancellor (1199-1202), h*eld it for the king in wardship for Helewisa's sons, Radulph and Ranulph.* Radulph being dead, and Ranulph remaining a

Kirk Gate, Middleham. Photograph 1906.

ward, the Archbishop Chancellor delivered up his entire wardship to Theobald de Valoynes; [6] and, during the whole of this period, it is to be observed that there were only twelve foresters and two *grassmani* — a sort of police, judging from their employment at Bainbridge — each of whom had two acres of land for ploughing between Goldmyresyke and the village. Their cattle were taken in every night for fear of the wolves. The duty of the Grassmani was to arrest malefactors in the forest and convey them to Richmond Castle." All this confirms the line of descent we have followed through Middleham and Spennithome. [7]

The interest of this book centers largely about the Castle of *Middleham* in Yorkshire, built by Robert Fitz Randolph in the latter part of the twelfth century. If time and space would permit, it would be interesting to linger about *Richmond* Castle, whose massive ruin is still to be seen nine miles from Middleham. Richmond was the seat of an Earldom before the Conquest. This "Honour" and the control which went with it was taken over by the Conqueror, and was conferred upon Alan, brother of Ribald, grandfather of Robert Fitz Randolph. Thus it came to be understood that the lands and titles and powers of this great Earldom, or Lordship, were "of the Honour of Richmond." Space is only taken here to give particular mention to the Gray Friars' Tower at Richmond, which is still to be seen as a reminder of the generosity and religious devotion of those who early bore this family name. Mr. Speight writes thus about this spot and memorial:

"Turning now from the market place through the old Friars' wynd, we arrive at the Tower of the Gray Friars, time-toned yet beautiful in decay. This house was of the foundation of one of the great Lords of Middleham, Ralph Fitz Randolph, in 1258. He died in 1270, and was buried at Coverham Abbey; but his heart, enclosed in a leaden urn, was interred in the choir of the Church of the Gray Friars of Richmond. He was a feudatory of the Earls of Richmond, and his place in the castle was over the Chapel of St. Nicholas on the East. In Gale's Registrum Honoris de Richmond there is a quaint old bird's-eye view of the castle; and over the oratory of St. Nicholas is portrayed a banner displaying the arms of the Fitz Randolphs; *or, a chief, indented, azure.*"

Church of St. Michael, the Archangel
Of which the Fitz Randolphs Were Patrons, and in which they found Sepulture, for several successive centuries.

Here, *again,* we find the Fitz Randolph arms, which, according to various authorities, already mentioned, have (as we venture to repeat) descended from a period now more than seven hundred years gone by. This heraldic device, after being thus borne by the Fitz Randolphs of Middleham, was, as we have seen, in the use of the Fitz Randolphs of Spennithorne for three hundred and fifty years or more, and was afterwards found (in substantially the same style) in the legitimate and authorized use of a Fitz Randolph of Nottinghamshire, the forefather of the Fitz Randolphs of Massachusetts and New Jersey. In St. Michael's Church at Spennithorne, the ancient burial place of the Fitz Randolphs is still found in the north aisle. Upon the altar-tomb of freestone are several armorial designs, emblazoned in their suitable heraldic colors. There are ten of these shields, of which four are Fitz Randolphs, all uniform, and corresponding to the coat-of-arms above given. Doubtless, upon the death of the head of the house, from time to time occurring, the family coat-of-arms was *again* placed upon this altar-tomb. The other coats-of-arms here represented are of families connected with, or descending from, the original Fitz Randolphs, namely, the Scropes, the Nevilles, and the Fitz Hughs.

Mr. Speight says that "Even before the Conqueror's great survey was made in 1086 the old free community of Spennithorne was a place with a history. It acquired an important standing; and, having been cultivated from a very early period, it had become a valuable possession at the time it was wrested from its then superior chief, Ghilpatric, who also ruled over Middleham. With Middleham it passed to the powerful Lord Ribald, brother of Alan, the first grantee of Richmondshire after the Conquest; and his posterity, the Fitz Randolphs, continued to hold the manor as of the Honour of Richmond by military service. They made Spennithorne their home for several centuries, and the foundations and part of the walls of their old manor house, since converted into cottages, are observable at the east end of the village... It is claimed by Cade that Spennithorne was a Roman station...St. Michael's Church occupies a sheltered, yet elevated, position; and from the top of its well-weathered tower is one of the loveliest views of the dale imaginable — the eye ranging over purple heath and wooded fell, and following for many miles the silvery windings of the Yore, by abbey, and castle, and stately hall, while many a beautiful village, hill, hamlet and tree-shaded-farm can be observed under the cheering influences of a bright sky."

If was the privilege of the writer to visit this ancient church and to verify Mr. Speight's descriptions and the coats-of-arms mentioned above; thence a drive was taken to the Shawl of Leyburn, a fine hill commanding an inspiring and delightful view of Wensleydale and of the imposing ruin of Middleham Castle.

An appreciative article, replete with tender reverence toward the past and its sacred traditions, appeared in the "Darlington and Stockton Times," April 29, 1905. This is a journal of much dignity and character, and is especially devoted to the interests of "Romantic Richmondshire," a portion only of whose charms can be touched upon in a book like this of ours. The article is entitled "Spennithorne Church," and in it constant reference is made to the patronage of the Fitz Randolphs through successive ages. This church is shown to be one of the very earliest in all Yorkshire, having been built, as we are informed, when the Conquest had not been accomplished more than one hundred years, and when the Normans were still busy erecting their strong castles and great churches. According to this article in the "Times" it was built by Robert Fitz Randolph in 1166. This date is probably correct; but, with all due deference to the author of the article, it seems probable that the builder of Spennithorne Oiurch was Ralph (or Randolph) the father of Robert, builder of Middleham Castle. In this article certain interesting records appear, to which, as yet, we have not adverted. It seems that, even prior to the date given, a Christian church existed at Spennithorne — which, in the great Domesday book, was called "Speningtorp." In "Domesday" there is an authentic record that "in Speningtorp, *Eccl est.* — i,e,, *there is a church,* or chapel. It is evident, says the writer in the "Times," that there *was a Saxon church* prior to the present structure, for stones with Runic characters have been found embedded in the east end of the chancel, and a Saxon cross sculptured upon a stone was discovered under the flags in the chancel during the restoration of about thirty-five years ago, and is now fixed in the wall in a dark comer of the vestry. The writer of the article has (from an imperfect list, to which he has had access, of rectors and patrons of "the living") brought forward some names of old-time interest. For example, in August, 1369, it appears that the patron of this church of St. Michael's the Archangel at Spennithorne was Matilda Fitz Randolph; and in July, 1433, the patron was Rad. Fitz Randolph — the first name of the patron, as given, probably being an abbreviation of Radulphus, otherwise Ralph or Randolph. After the marriage of the Fitz Randolphs with the Wyvills we find this last name repeatedly among the patrons, and, every now and then, associated with the Scroopes (or Scropes) of Danby. In 1551, for example, Christopher Wyvill was patron of the church; and it was about this same time, as we may recall, that his relative, Christopher Fitz Randolph, was filling a place of social prominence a little way southward in Nottinghamshire. [8] Again in 1649 the family of Wyvill was associated with the patronage of the church, and in 1672 another Christopher Wyvill, Bart., was associated with William Wyvill, Gent., in the patronage of the church; and in 1729 Sir Marmaduke Wyvill, Bart., was the patron; and in 1764 Sir M. A. Wyvill, Bart., was patron. One of the rectors of the church was Rev. Francis Wyvill, who filled this position from 1615 to 1625, and an oil portrait of him is still to be seen at the rectory at Spennithorne. We quote below some interesting lines from this well-considered article in the Darlington and Stockton "Times":

"In that chamber which now contains the organ, at the end of the north aisle, there will be observed a curious tombstone, like a stone chest against the wall, with a plain surface. There is no inscription on it, but it has sculptured around its sides in relief, representations of heraldic shields painted in their appropriate colors, which during the last restoration were probably renewed. Fortunately there has been preserved a will which determines who is the tenant of this nameless grave. The copy of the testament of Alan Fitz Randolph, dated 1457, directs that his body be interred in the Church of St. Michael the Archangel, of Spenningthorn, in the chapel of St. Mary.' This chamber, then the chapel of St. Mary, as it is still called, was evidently the burial place of this ancient family of Fitz Randoph. These armorial shields are of the following: 1st, Fitz Randolph; 2d, Scroope of Masham; 3d, Gules, saltire, arg.; 4th, two bars, az.; 5th, Fitz Randolph; 6th,...7th, Scroope of Harden; 8th, Fitz Randolph; 9th, Fitz Hugh; 10th, Fitz Randolph.

"The chantry was a chapel, or part of a Catholic church, endowed to support a priest to chant mass daily or periodically for the dead, and it appears from an ancient record that the chantry in Spennithorne Church was in use in the time of Henry VIII, and Richard Marshall was then the priest. The record states that the priest ordained was 'Richard Marshall of the ordynnaunce of Jno. Fitz Randoll, Esquyer, to the intent to pray for his soul, his ffrendes' soules, and all Xtian soules as apperyth by a copy of ded af ffeofment made to Xofer [9] Conyer, sune and heyre apparent to Willm. Lord Conyers, date XX mo. Januarii, ann. Reg. K. Henry VIII, XI. The same is wythyn the said churche. The necessitie is to pray for the soule of the ffounder and all Xtian soules; and the same is observed and kepte accordingly, and the same is under charge ffor payment of the ffirste frutes and tenths.'

"A fresco is on the wall near the chief entrance door. It is a representation of Old Time, about 10 ft. high; in his right hand, the symbolic scythe; in his left, the hourglass; on his brow, the forelock. Although this fresco has been whitewashed again and again during three centuries. Old Time has refused to be wiped out, and has always come out again, till simple folk have begun to have a kind of weird and superstitious idea about him, as if he were something uncanny, and better let alone.

"So in this small church in rural Wensleydale we have the memorials of an historic and distant past, and also of a vast Empire, showing that even from this quiet spot Britain's sons have gone forth with distinction to distant parts of the world, and done good service. Even this small church is eloquent with the consecration of the past; and as we stand in its chancel alone, the mural tablets, the emblazoned windows, in memory of the brave, the pious, and beautiful — the light playing through the stained windows in gules, azure, and vert as in still melody — all speak eloquently to the heart things unutterable, 'thoughts that wander through eternity.' 'Sic transit gloria mundi,' says grim Old Time, there. 'Aye,' Faith replies, 'earthly glory, but there is an immortal.'"

[1] It will be remembered that Henry II was contemporary with Robert of Middleham, who, with his sons, were castle-builders and monastery-builders and church-builders. The chevrons and chevronels, which came on certain

coats of arms in the days of the Second and Third Henrys, were named from their resemblance to the main rafters or principals of a roof, a familiar sight in early buildings. The Fitz Hughs, descended from Henry Fitz Randolph, Lord of Ravensworth, bore on their arms chevronels. Otherwise their shield (as well as that of the famous High Sheriff of Henry II) resembled that of the Fitz Randolphs of Spennithorne.

It is not impossible that the "indent" of the "chief" (which is the top of the shield) is a modification of the chevronel.

[2] The Romans appear to have called the river *Urus* — as having at times a fierceness and fury like that of a mad bull. The Saxons callea it Jore, or Yore. From it the city of York was named. "Jervaulx Abbey" presents an extreme of etymological transformation. It was the Abbey of the Vale of the Yore.

[3] Going back to Ribald, Lord of Middleham, and progenitor of the Fitz Randolph line, we find in the "Dormant and Extinct Baronage of England," published just a century ago by T. C Banks, that his coat of arms was "O, on a chief, indented, az. A Lion passant of the First."

[4] Barker remarks, in a note at page 127 of his "History of Wensleydale:" "The change of supporters and badges is, strictly speaking, chiefly *dependent upon the will of the bearer; and so likewise of crests and mottoes...But no man may change his paternal shield, though entitled to slightly difference it without a confirmation;* and he must on no account usurp the arms of another." The writer has seen a different coat-of-arms claimed as belonging to the Fitz Randolphs and to which was attached the inspiring motto "Jamais arriere." It has been found impossible to trace this to any authentic source.

[5] As a recent possible exception to this, a fact mentioned by Mr. Speight may be cited — "The late Mr. Wyville," he writes, "claimed the Baronetcy of Scrope of Masham, which was in abeyance between his family and that of the late Mr. Wm. Danby, of Swinton Park." — Romantic Rich., page 342.

[6] So far as we can know, their Lordships faithfully administered upon their trust; but for fully five hundred years following the Conquest great estates constituted rich feeding ground for administrators and for the appointing sovereign. Hume says that when a baron died the king took possession, and the heir applied and made homage and paid a composition to the king. If the heir were a minor the king had the income during the minority. "When the king granted the wardship of a rich heir to any one, he had the opportunity of enriching a favorite or minister; if he sold it. he thereby levied a considerable sum of money. Simon de Montfort said Henry III ten thousand marks for the wardship of Gilbert d'Umfreville. Geoffrey de Mandeville paid to the same prince twenty thousand marks that he might marry Isabel, Countess of Gloucester, and possess her lands. If the heir were a female, the king was entitled to offer her any husband of her rank he thought proper. It she refused, she forfeited her land." — Hume I, p. 476.

[7] Still another of these curious old thirteenth century controversies is brought forward by Gale on page 90 of his Registrum. It is a claim of Randolph Fitz Randolph for free forestry or hunting at the Manor property of

Wodhall. Randolph is here rendered in the old Latin text as Radulphus and at the top of the page is printed in beautiful red type the title to his claim, viz., "Clameum Rad. F. Ranulphi." Here we find perhaps a sort of precedent for those of us who in New Jersey substitute the initial F. for the prefix Fitz.

[8] The persistence in the kinship of this somewhat unusual name, from the time it enters the family soon after the marriage with the daughter of John of Gaunt, is at least remarkable. It was afterwards in use in the first generation of Fitz Randolphs after their settlement in New Jersey. But of this name and its associations more will appear further on.

[9] In the fifteenth and sixteenth centuries the name Christopher was usually written thus — Xofer, or Xpofer.

Church of St. Wilfrid, Kirkby-In-Ashfield, Nottinghamshire
In which was found the tablet commemorating Certain of the Fitz Randolphs of the Sixteenth Century. Photographed 1906. A few months later this church and its contents were destroyed by fire.

Chapter Seven - Kirkby, Sutton and Langton Hall

In the northwestern part of Nottinghamshire are two towns about three miles apart: one of them being called Kirkby-in-Ashfield, and the other being known as Suttonin-Ashfield. At Kirkby-in-Ashfield a church has existed from the days of St. Wilfrid. The edifice has from time to time been restored, and, since the visit made to it by the writer in 1906, it has been destroyed by fire; and, so far as he is aware, its contents were also destroyed. He found upon its wall an interesting memorial of the Fltz Randolph family. The fact of its existence had been brought to his attention by his daughter [1] who had visited this church in 1896, and had copied the language of this memorial. The writer compared the copy with the original, in 1906, and found it accurate. It is as follows:

"Hie jacent corpora Thomae Fitzrandolf nuper de
"Langton Hall huius parochiae generosi et Katharinae
"uxoris eius quorum patres fuere X pofer Fitzran
"dolf nuper de Langton predicta armiger et God
"fratus Fulliambe nuper de Walton Hall in Com.
 "Darby miles. Animae illorum petiere astra.
"Predicta Katharinae obiit 2° Mali A.D. 1593
"et predict Thomae 27 die Februarii 1598."

The translation of the above appears below:

"Here lie the bodies of Thomas Fitzrandolph, late of
"Langton Hall, gentleman, of this parish, and of
"Katherine, his wife, whose fathers were Christopher
"Fitzrandolph, Squire, of Langton aforesaid, and
"Godfrey Fulliambe, Knight, late of Walton Hall
"in the County of Darby. Their spirits sought
"the stars. Said Katherine died May 2, A.D. 1593,
"and said Thomas Feb. 27, 1598."

The writer is informed that this brass tablet was discovered about thirty years ago by the Rev. T. Woodman, incumbent of Kirkby, whilst digging in his garden, adjoining the churchyard — which presumably in earlier years included this garden. The reverend gentleman took counsel with his warden, Col. William Langton Coke, as to what disposition should be made of the tablet, at the same time expressing some doubt or aversion as to the line about "the stars." Col. Coke very suitably advised the vicar to place the tablet on the church wall, and it was so done.

The church of St. Mary Magdalene at Sutton-in-Ashfield has records reaching back to the time when such records were instituted under the reign of Henry VIII; but these sixteenth century records were crude, and in the register at Sutton they are more or less confused and in disorder. A recent attempt to bind them together has not been wholly successful. They furnish, however, data of some value and of considerable interest.

We learn from them that at some time in the month of June, 1588, "X Pofer Fitz randoll" was there buried. This doubtless was Christopher Fitz Randolph, Esquire, of Langton Hall. The eldest son of Christopher was Thomas, whose name appears in the brass tablet, and who married the daughter of Sir Godfrey Fulliambe, or, as Thoroton spells it, Folijambe. It appears that Thomas had a son. Jacobus (or James), who married a daughter of a distinguished Northampton family, and they had a son, Philalethes, or Philalerhes, who died at twenty-two without issue. Other sons of Christopher were John and Edward and Christopher. All of these were of Langton Hall, a charming old mansion situated about two miles from Kirkby-in-Ashfield, and having a tradition and record flavored with antiquity even when Thoroton wrote of it in 1677. From Thoroton we learn that "John Langton of Kirkeby about the nineth year of Henry VI held when he died one Mess. [2] called Langton Place and six closes."

Parish Church, Sutton-In-Ashfield,
St. Mary Magdalene.

Thoroton traces back the record of Langton Hall to the time of Henry III (middle of thirteenth century), and to the possession of Richard de Ruddington, and says in effect that from this early ownership it was conveyed to Geoffrey de Langton. "In Langton's family it continued till Henry the Eighth's time — that Cuthbert Langton, dying without issue male, it fell to Fitz Randolph by the marriage of Langton's daughter and heir, in whose name it continued till of late."

It was the privilege of the writer and his companion to visit Langton Hall in 1906, and to enjoy in it an example of the generous and gracious hospitality which has doubtless for many centuries been there dispensed. For a number of years it has been in the ownership of the family of Admiral Salmond, and has had the most considerate care. The mansion is long and low, with quaint old rooms and charming antique windows and arches, and opens out to a well-kept driveway and to the perfection of an English lawn; and close by we entered a rose garden of the sort rarely found away from the Isles of Britain. No wonder that when the spirits of its favored occupants, in the ages agone, could no longer linger here, they "sought the stars."

Thoroton informs us that "in 1612 the owners of Sutton-in-Ashfield are set down, William, Lord Cavendish, Edward Langford, Thomas Clark, William Lyndtey of Skegby, Gent., and Edward Fitz Randolph, Gent."

Langton Hall. Photograph 1906.

It appears that this Edward Fitz Randolph, a younger brother of Thomas of the brass tablet, had several children, whose names are given (with sundry vagaries of orthography and other uncertainties) in the tattered records of the church at Sutton. Prodding amongst these memorials, we learn that Elizabeth, daughter to Edward, was baptized November 17, 1589; that "Richard Fitzrando, sonne of Edward," was baptized in August, 1596 (precise date not given); and that "Edward Fitzrandall, Sonne of Edward Fitzrandal," was baptized the 17th day of July, 1607.

It has been well understood that Edward Fitz Randolph, the father of the New Jersey Fitz Randolphs, was born in Nottinghamshire about the beginning of the seventeenth century. Nathaniel Fitz Randolph in his "Book of Records" (1750) writes positively of Nottinghamshire as the locality whence Edward emigrated, but does not fix his birth-date. Some (including Nathaniel Fitz Randolph) have *supposed* this to be about 1614, but as to this there is no certainty. Considering the confused way in which the church records at Sutton were kept and preserved, it is by no means impossible that a slight inaccuracy may have crept into them regarding the exact time of the birth of this Edward, who was the son of Edward and the grandson of Christopher Fitz Randolph of Langton Hall. The precise data are not at hand to correct either the tradition (or supposition) as to date, which has been held in the family on the one hand, or to qualify the ancient church record on the other. The difference in years would be short and is in no way important. [3] We do know that the emigrant Edward of Nottinghamshire was barely, if quite, grown up when he came to Massachusetts in 1630, and that he was still quite a young man when he married Elizabeth Blossom at Scituate, Mass., on the 10th of May, 1637, and this is consistent with the information contained in the Sutton records; and in these records we find practical confirmation of the "book" of Nathaniel and of the facts and traditions handed down in the family since Pilgrim days.

[1] Then Miss Caroline Fitz Randolph; now the wife of Dr. Charles D. Parfitt of Ontario.
[2] *Messuage* — a manor house and its appendages.
[3] Enjoying an excellent dinner at the ancient "Denman's Head" of Sutton, at which presided Mine Host Keeley — who, if he had not chanced to be an Irishman, would have been a veritable Sam Johnson of an Englishman for dominating talkativeness and wit — I asked our eloquent landlord how old his inn might be. He replied that he was not there to start it and couldn't be certain, but it might be five hundred years old. I mused aloud that I had an impression of having lived there some three hundred years back. "Is that all?" queried the wide-eyed but skeptical Benedict. "Well," I rejoined, "it might be four hundred years." "Ye remoind me." said the innkeeper, "of a

shnortsman who tould a frind that he'd joust snot nointynoine crowa. His irind asked him — 'cuddent he make it a hundred?' 'No. I cuddent,' says he, 'do ye think I'd tell a lie for a CROW?'"

Chapter Eight - The Fitz Randolph House as Conjoined with the Westmoreland House

At this point let us retrace our steps so far as to return to the descendants of Radulphus (or Ralph, or Randolph) de Neville, Earl of Westmoreland, who died in the fourth year of King Henry VI, that is, in the year 1435We have followed his line by his second wife, Joan of Beaufort, to and through the royal line of Great Britain from the fifteenth century to the twentieth. We now return to the line of descent from his first wife, Margery, Lady Stafford. This may be called the senior line. We have seen that this Randolph, the husband of Margery, was the Earl of Westmoreland; and the Earldom, or, more correctly speaking, the Dukedom -of Westmoreland, descends in the line of primogeniture to his posterity. His oldest son was Radulphus, or Randolph; but Randolph's children were all daughters and the Dukedom descended through his brother John, who married Elizabeth, daughter of Thomas Holland, Earl of Canterbury. Their son was John, who was hero of the famous fight at Towton in the first year of Edward IV, and who married Anna, the widow of a near relative. Their son was Randolph, or Ralph, Duke of Westmoreland, who married Margery Booth of Barton of a noble Lancaster family. Their only son, again, was Ralph, or Randolph, whose wife's name was Edith. Their son was another Ralph, or Randolph, who held the Dukedom of Westmoreland, and who married Catherine, daughter of Edward, Duke of Buckingham, and died in the fifteenth year of Henry VIII. Ralph and Catherine had a large family — the larger proportion being daughters. Of the sons we shall shortly make further mention in some detail. The oldest son was Henry, Duke of Westmoreland, who died in the fifth year of Elizabeth's reign. Henry had two wives, by the second of whom, Margery, he had two daughters; but by the first, Jane, who was daughter of Thomas, Earl of Rutland, he had (besides four daughters) a son, Charles, who was the last Duke of Westmoreland, and who married Anna, daughter of Henry, Duke of Surrey. Their offspring consisted of four daughters. This last duke, Charles, was attainted for his opposition to the rule of Elizabeth when refusing to obey the summons to her presence, issued to him and to his kinsman, the Duke of Northumberland, in 1571. Afterwards he sought shelter amongst the Scotch Borderers, and made his way to the Continent, where the remainder of his life was spent. His dukedom and his properties were confiscated to the Crown.

We have referred to the large family of the last Ralph, or Randolph, Duke of Westmoreland, whose wife was Catherine and whose oldest son was Henry, the father of Charles. *Henry's brothers* appear to have been *Thomas, Edward, Christopher, Randolph and Cuthbert.* Christopher is mentioned as having been present at the family council at Raby Castle when the reply of refusal was sent up to Queen Elizabeth.

The writer has been unable to ascertain, through Gale or otherwise, the particulars of birth, death and marriage of these several brothers of Henry, Duke of Westmoreland. As we have already seen, Henry himself died in the fifth year of Queen Elizabeth, that is, in the year 1563. It is probable that the whole period of his brothers' lives may have been, say, between 1500 and 1570, covering the entire reign of Henry VIII, and, perhaps, antedating and postdating that reign somewhat. Now, it was, as we recall, in the thirtieth year of King Henry VIIFs reign that Christopher Fitz Randolph (according to Blackner's History) took part in a "perambulation of the fforest of Sheerewood." We have learned from the Church Records at Sutton that Christopher Fitz Randolph was there buried in 1588. Just here, exact, positive history would seem to pause. The writer is without absolute proof in record-form that Christopher Fitz Randolph, who died in 1588, was the son of Thomas, or of Edward, or of Christopher, or of Cuthbert, [1] or of Randolph, who appear to have been the brothers of Henry, Duke of Westmoreland. There is, however, evidence (and some of it has been quite abundantly adduced in the course of this narrative) that Christopher and Thomas and Edward Fitz Randolph of the Sutton Records and of the Thoroton Antiquities (and as to two of them— of the memorial mural tablet at Kirkby) were of the same line and source and heraldry as was not only the Spennithome line but also the original line of the Lords of Middleham from whom were descended the Earls of Westmoreland. One remarkable thing in this situation is the *juxtaposition* of names and dates under circumstances which appear plainly to indicate, if not to establish, this trio of names — Christopher and Thomas and Edward of the Westmoreland succession as closely related to a corresponding trio of names in the Nottinghamshire line, and to indicate as the strongest of probabilities, amounting, as it would appear, to a moral certainty, that one of the five brothers of Henry, Duke of Westmoreland (namely, Thomas, Edward, Christopher, Randolph and Cuthbert) was the progenitor of this group of names already encountered in Thoroton's Records, in Kirkby Church and in Sutton Church — namely, Christopher, Thomas and Edward Fitz Randolph.

In passing, it may here be noted (in relation to the remark as to lack of record-evidence) that, aside from the accumulations of historian or antiquarian, no such particular evidence could possibly have come down to us; for all church records of England begin a full generation (or more) later than the appearance in life of the sons of this last Randolph of the Earls of Westmoreland. But the juxtaposition above mentioned includes the fact that the treasured annals of two distinguished antiquarians, who may also be called historians (both of whom give much attention and space to Fitz Randolph lines), meet at this point — Gale, whose story is chiefly of Yorkshire, bringing down to a point of interest from the most ancient days of Norman conquest and glory a single continuous genealogical tale, and ending it with the names of Christopher, Thomas, Edward, Randolph and Cuthbert, whilst Thoroton, the antiquary of Nottinghamshire (though the date of publication of his "antiquities" is slightly earlier) apparently takes up the story with the same names and carries it forward for some generations; and meanwhile to us this story is further illuminated by the earliest of the church records, by a church memorial tablet, and by other circumstances of interest

Now let us see for a moment what are the circumstances indicating that the next of kin of the Duke of Westmoreland would revert to the ancient family name and hold the coat-of-arms of the Fitz Randolphs from whom the Westmorelands had descended.

Incidentally, we may here bear in mind that the name and house of Neville was itself an adoption or a transplantation. Gilbert Neville, a Norman, had come in the train of William the Conqueror to England. A great granddaughter of his, Isabelle, had married Robert, a descendant of the Fitz Maldreds of Saxon lineage. At this point, the *Fitz Maldreds* abandoned their own family name and accepted that of the wife. Robert's son, Galfridus, or Geoffrey, therefore, instead of writing himself a Fitz Maldred, took the name of Neville; and this continued through more than a dozen generations, stretching from the end of the twelfth century to the middle of the sixteenth. One abandonment of a family name would perhaps make another all the easier and the more natural, if such abandonment should appear advisable or desirable.

Moreover, the greatest glory and the largest advantage which appeared to have come to the Nevilles was through the marriage of Mary Fitz Randolph of Middleham to Robert de Neville about the middle of the thirteenth century. Still further, the family name of Fitz Randolph was one of decidedly greater distinction and was allied with more ability, prestige and success than either Neville or Fitz Maldred. And, again still further, Thomas and Edward and Christopher and Cuthbert and Randolph, the brothers of Henry, Duke of Westmoreland, were themselves in a peculiar and strict sense Fitz Randolphs. Their father's name was Randolph. *His* father's name was Randolph. His father's name was Randolph, or, as the name is frequently written in an abbreviated form, Ralph, or, as given by Gale and other writers in their Latin records, Radulphus.

Moreover still, in the line of descent from Ribald, the brother of the great Alan (trusted lieutenant of William the Conqueror), in the course of about four centuries of this line of worthies, there were no less than twelve Randolphs in the family headship. In other words, *nearly* all of the sons, who were in the line of primogeniture either of the Fitz Randolphs or of the earlier Nevilles or of the Earls of Westmoreland, were Randolphs.

For all these reasons, if there were any occasion at all to change again the family patronym, it would be the most reasonable and natural and dignified thing possible to fall back upon the designation, which had been a word of power and preference, not only through the entire history of the English commonwealth from the time of the Conqueror downward, but also even in Brittany and Normandy and Norseland long before William the Norman's invasion was dreamt of.

But what circumstance was there which would suggest or induce any change of name by the kinship of the Westmorelands? There were perhaps two considerations, the second being the stronger. The first arose by reason of the parting of the ways at the second marriage of the Ralph, or Randolph, whose second wife was the celebrated Joan of Beaufort. [2] His first wife. Lady Stafford, it has been seen, was of noble, and even of royal, descent, and her children constituted the older and perhaps the prouder division; and yet Joan Beaufort was also of royal blood, and amongst Joan's immediate posterity there are many names of great strength and high repute; and, incidentally, it may at this point be remarked that the names which are associated with our Massachusetts and New Jersey line of Fitz Randolph, and which appear in Thoroton and in Kirkby and in Sutton, as already shown, are names which had descended on Joan's side of the family of the Ralph of Westmoreland, who died in 1435. Amongst *Joan's* numerous children are three — named Edward, Cuthbert and Thomas.

Although as pointed out by recent histories, there may have been to some extent a separation in feeling and interest between these two divisions of the family, still, it is to be said that in public matters and in religious views they usually kept close to the old lines and standards, and so kept together. They were Catholics, but they had been Lancastrians, and they would have gladly been Catholics of the Wycliffe or Lancastrian school — Catholics of the open mind — of liberal views— of progressive principles. They lamented the threatened disintegration of the Catholic Church; but what they most abhorred was the substitution therefor of the personal autocracy of the Tudors. In one or two exceptional cases the Tudors came into close touch and relationship with the Nevilles and Westmorelands; but, for the most part, the principles of these parties were as far apart as the poles. The old Fitz Randolph blood and mind had scant sympathy for Tudor greediness, and less respect for Tudor doctrines and tyranny. Henry VII was a usurper. He had no proper place in royalty. By the ancient families he was regarded as a parvenu and common adventurer. He proved himself at once a man of ability, but also a tyrant and a miser. He seized what he could of other people's possessions and hoarded them. His son, Henry VIII, was even more greedy — whilst he changed his father's policy of parsimonious acquisition into a policy of lavish expenditure for self-gratification. His father's wealth and the royal allowances made by his people sufficed not to provide for his costly folly and sin. He desired more wives than the Catholic religion would permit. Two things therefore became apparently necessary to him, namely, to dissolve the monasteries and despoil the religious institutions of his country in order to supply funds to meet his personal extravagances and to set up a church of which he should be high priest and sole ruler.

All this was detested by the Westmorelands. One after another they sought to disallow and oppose, as best they might, the Tudor type of tyranny and irreligion. One after another the Nevilles and Westmorelands went down before the Tudor axe and power. Of the line of Joan of Beaufort, the Salisburys, the Nevilles and the Latimers suffered the terrible consequences of uttering even whispers against the royalty of their time. The persecutions continued through the days of all the Tudor sovereigns. The saddest picture in that series of horrors is the murder in 1541 of the Countess of Salisbury, I call it by that name because it seems to have known no other. Even Froude, the apologist for the Tudors, so characterizes it. The aged countess was not brought to trial — she was sentenced to death by attainder, and was held as a close prisoner in the Tower for a year; and then, on May 27, 1541, the very day on which Sir John Neville was executed at York, the Countess of Salisbury was chased about the fatal green within the tower by Henry's executioner; and, refusing with lofty dignity to submit her neck to the axe, was brutally killed. Of all this Froude writes — "The offence of the aged countess, even though it could be proved to have been deliberate, constructive treason, would appear still too little to palliate or even explain her death. A murder, though unpremeditated, remains among the few acts to which modern sentiment refuses indulgence." [3]

Prior to this, on the 9th of December, 1538, Sir Edward Neville, together with Lord Montague and the Marquis of Exeter, had been beheaded on Tower Hill for treason against Henry on evidence which in our day would be regarded as utterly insignificant. In the case of Sir John Neville and a few others executed with him, the crime committed was chiefly the asserting of the rights of the priests to the refuge they had obtained with the Scottish borderers. As the historian tells us, they had not fought a battle nor taken a life. During the period of Mary Tudor's rule, the Nevilles and Westmorelands were, being Catholics, less troubled; but it appears that, even with the Duke of Westmoreland, his Catholicity was not of that Spanish inquisitorial type most affected by Mary. He and several other nobles were put under suspicion by Mary as to the soundness of their religion, and they were reprimanded for holding views not acceptable to the Catholic queen. Is it any wonder that, following all these sorrows and sufferings of the Nevilles and Westmorelands — and of their posterity and kinsmen the Salisburys and Dacres and Latimers, — Charles, Duke of Westmoreland should in Elizabeth's day find himself driven from further allegiance to Tudor dominance. Even he approached the reality of disloyalty reluctantly; but, when Queen Elizabeth sent for him (and the heads of other noble families), demanding that he should appear before her to answer for himself, he, after a family council, determined to disobey the queen. Being attainted, his splendid property was confiscated, his titles of nobility were obliterated, and his family name was apparently stained with the disgrace of treason. [4]

The Westmoreland dislike of the Tudors antedated the sufferings just now briefly outlined. Henry Tudor, before he became King Henry VII, had taken the title of Duke of Richmond — a title which had first been borne by the great Alan Rufus, the brother of Ribald, ancestor of the Westmorelands. Worse than this — when Henry VIII desired to advance his bastard son, to whom his mistress, Elizabeth Blount gave birth in 1519, he made this illegitimate offspring Duke of Richmond, a title which in earlier days had been held in highest respect and reverence by the Westmorelands and other descendants of the companions of the Conqueror.

It is quite true that some of the later events I have recounted took place at dates later than the appearance, as Fitz Randolphs of men who, so far as we can reasonably judge, must have come out of the line of Westmoreland; and the writer has no wish to force the argument as to any possible occasion for a readoption of the old family name. He has continued the Westmoreland story down to the attainder (by Queen Elizabeth) of the last duke to show that the old indignation persisted to the end and to place in evidence its final results. Suffice it to say that the Westmorelands had a continuing feud with the Tudors, and were gradually and effectually crushed by them.

Now as to the junior members of the family connection — those who were not in any case in the direct line of title and wealth, and whose only inheritance would have been character and the distinction attaching to a noble ancestry, — it is of all things the most natural that they should, under existing circumstances, grieve at the calamities which befell their name and house. So lamenting, what better, nobler, or more suitable thing could they do than to assume — as they had every right to do — the name of the ancient family from which much of their glory had been originally derived, and which name had been kept so persistently before them in the headship of each generation for nearly four centuries? [5]

But in the case of the assumption by the descendants of the dukes of Westmoreland, or by any of them of the ancient and honored name of Fitz Randolph, there would be even *no such change* of name as when the Fitz Maldreds took over the name of Neville. [6] In fact, the name of Fitz Randolph had always been one of the appellations, or titles, or properties of the House, and a reversion to it — either by a senior or by a junior branch — would at any time have been a normal proceeding.

Once more, in this particular case, there was *doubtless no change at all* — and not even a formal reversion to an ancient type or form; for, taking all the circumstances together, there is hardly room for question concerning the descent of Christopher and the two following Edwards and their Massachusetts and New Jersey posterity *directly from Randolph, 5th son of the Duke of Westmoreland of the time of Henry VIII.* Any son of this Randolph would necessarily be a Fitz Randolph, the meaning of the name being precisely that. The brothers of the duke first mentioned, in the order as named by Gale, are (1) Henry (who inherited the title), (2) Thomas, (3) Edward, (4) Christopher, (5) Randolph, (6) Cuthbert.

This section of this logical and genealogical line would then appear as shown on following page.

Recapitulated briefly, therefore, and taken at a glance, the Fitz Randolphs of the sixteenth and seventeenth centuries, whose particular line we are following, would stand thus:

Randolph (Duke of Westmoreland).
Randolph (5th son of the Duke).
Christopher Fitz Randolph.
Edward Fitz Randolph.
Edward Fitz Randolph, the Pilgrim.

Thoroton and Blackner have introduced us to a young gentleman of quality named Christopher Fitz Randolph who, in the latter part of the long reign of Henry VIII, assisted at the "perambulacion" of Sherwood Forest The Sutton Church register and the Kirkby Church Memorial tablet have presented us to Christopher's sons, Thomas and Edward (the former being wed to the daughter of a baronet of ancient lineage), and Thoroton again comes in with his genealogical tables showing that the line of Thomas was extinguished in the second subsequent generation, but mentioning (besides a Christopher and a John) an Edward Fitz Randolph, who undoubtedly is the same mentioned in the .Sutton register as the father of another Edward — born in the first decade of the seventeenth century — which last, we are well convinced, was Edward the Pilgrim.

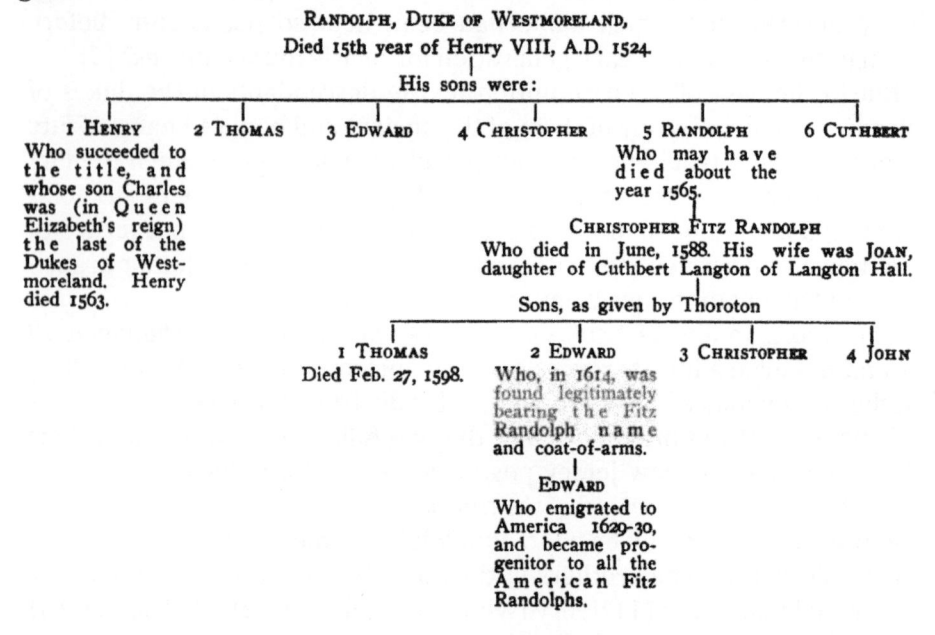

RANDOLPH, DUKE OF WESTMORELAND,
Died 15th year of Henry VIII, A.D. 1524.

His sons were:

1 HENRY	2 THOMAS	3 EDWARD	4 CHRISTOPHER	5 RANDOLPH	6 CUTHBERT
Who succeeded to the title, and whose son Charles was (in Queen Elizabeth's reign) the last of the Dukes of Westmoreland. Henry died 1563.				Who may have died about the year 1565.	

CHRISTOPHER FITZ RANDOLPH
Who died in June, 1588. His wife was JOAN, daughter of Cuthbert Langton of Langton Hall.

Sons, as given by Thoroton

1 THOMAS	2 EDWARD	3 CHRISTOPHER	4 JOHN
Died Feb. 27, 1598.	Who, in 1614, was found legitimately bearing the Fitz Randolph name and coat-of-arms.		

EDWARD
Who emigrated to America 1629-30, and became progenitor to all the American Fitz Randolphs.

The Tudors, the incoming of whom brought such disaster and sorrow to the family whose history we have followed, gained the English throne four centuries ago. In those days comparatively few of the English surnames now heard were chosen or settled in families. For the most part only nobles had enjoyed family names of persistence and significance. Even these we have seen to shift and change as occasion required. Afterward names were chosen or became fixed by reason of occupations — of personal peculiarity — of demeanor — or achievement — or of some extraordinary event, or as connected with some particular locality. Fitz Randolph was not of these. It had from early centuries been a persistent and honored name. It had never been in wide or general use. It was not difficult to trace those who had borne it. In one spot alone in upper Yorkshire it had continued for several centuries. Its coat-of-arms was continuous and was in recognized use by Edward Fitz Randolph in Stuart days, just following Tudor days. Eliminating the brief lines of the Lord of Ravensworth and the High Sheriff of Henry II — both of whom had been merged in other names and families for centuries gone by — there was *no other line* to which Christopher Fitz Randolph could belong than that which descended from the Lords of Middleham. Finding his son, Edward, father of Edward the Pilgrim, bearing the coat-of-arms of this noble line, there seems to be no escape from our conclusion that the Nottinghamshire and American Fitz Randolphs came down from this junior branch of Westmoreland. The combined testimony of antiquarian, of church register and of mural tablet alike point to this conclusion. Many circumstances join to establish it. The coincidence of several "christened" names, beginning some generations earlier in the kinship, and continuing to and into the American posterity confirm it. The arms verify it and the dates precisely fit it. Such a concatenation can find no other explication. It appears safe to say that Christopher Fitz Randolph, the grandfather of Edward the Pilgrim, could have derived his name from no other line than this. Here and not elsewhere do we find a fit setting for his name, his associations and his marriage with the heiress of Langton Hall.

[1] Noting this name Cuthbert more than once in the Neville and Westmoreland records, and again noting it in the name of Cuthbert Langton, of Langton, Hall (whose daughter Christopher Fitz Randolph married) a query arises as to the possibility of this having been a marriage of relatives, or of family connections. Cuthbert was an unusual name. It had association with the family of Percy of Northumberland, with whom in relationship, religion and friendship the Nevilles were united. This is one of the minor coincidences of our story, but apparently not without interest.

[2] Roger Gale continues in his ancient Latin record the name Neville from point to point along down through the lines of descendants of Joan Beaufort but never once gives the name Neville as the name of any descendant of Lady Stafford, though he follows the Westmoreland line down to the daughters of Charles, the last duke. We have not found the quintette of brothers of Henry. Duke of Westmoreland, mentioned otherwheres than by Gale: and by him neither Thomas nor Edward, nor Christopher, nor Randolph, nor Cuthbert is said to be a Neville. Westmoreland was a dukedom — not a family name. By what family name should the younger brothers of the duke and their sons be known?

[3] Over the death of Lord Dacres, another connection of the Nevilles, Froude sheds more historical tears than over that of the ill-fated and high-charactered countess. Dacres had inadvertently fallen into a fracas whilst hunting deer in which a forester had been killed. His participation in the affray would hardly have incurred a death sentence in any age. But Henry was determined on his death against reason and intercession alike, and to the scaffold the popular young nobleman accordingly was led.

[4] History has but one voice and verdict touching the character and proud position of this noble duke. Froude writes of him and his comrade in opposition to Tudor rule (the Duke of Northumberland) as "the hereditary leaders of the North." "The Earl of Westmoreland," says Froude, "was the head of the great House of Neville, from a younger branch of which had sprung Warwick, the King-maker. He was the great-grandson of Stafford, Duke of Buckingham. He had married a sister of the Duke of Norfolk. No shield in England showed

prouder quarterings, and no family had played a grander part in the feudal era of England?' — Froude's History of Eng., Vol. IX, 517. Hume says "The great credit of these two noblemen [Westmoreland and Northumberland], with that zeal for the Catholic religion which still prevailed, soon drew together multitudes." — Hume's History of England III, 881.

[5] Of course the writer does not intimate the possibility in any case of a change of name by all the Nevilles. There are still Nevilles m England, and the writer has met some in America.

[6] A like circumstance had diversified the history of the Percies, Earls of Northumberland and of Worcester, of whom Gairdner writes, "Not one of the English noble houses is so distinguished as the Percies throughout the whole range of English history. It is remarkable alike for its long unbroken line, its high achievements, its general culture of arts and of letters. Pre-eminent also, as remarked by Sir Harris Nicolas, for its alliances among the peerage, it continues to this day, *though represented once more by a female branch.*" The earlier event here alluded to took place in the reign of Henry II when William de Perci's male descendants became extinct, and Agnes, the daughter from whom all subsequent Percies descended, accepted as her husband Josceline, a son of Geoffrey. Duke of Louvain, on the express condition that he and his posterity should bear the surname of Percy. If our line as ultimately drawn in this book be found correct it will be observed that these Percies are in the Fitz Randolph ancestry. The mother of the first Earl of Westmoreland was Matilda Percy, and William, Lord Percy, had preceded her in the alliance.

Chapter Nine - Review of Line of Descent from Rolf the Norseman to Edward the Pilgrim

Here, then, once more the writer pauses to recapitulate his ascertainments and conclusions. To the following ancestral story — here given in merest outline — any American Fitz Randolph, who has been at the trouble of tracing his lineage back to Edward the Pilgrim, may, we believe, safely and reasonably link his line.

(1) **Rolf** — The Norseman Conqueror.
Born about A.D. 860. Died A.D. 932. Married Gisela, daughter of King Charles of France.
(2) **William, "Longsword"** — Duke of Normandy.
Died about 943.
(3) **Richard "The Fearless"** — Duke of Normandy.
Reigned more than half a century. Died A.D. 996.
(4) **Richard "The Good"** — Duke of Normandy. Died A.D. 1026.
(5) **Richard** — Duke of Normandy.

Whose wife was Judith. He died A.D. 1028. [He was father of Robert "The Magnificent," whose son was William "The Conqueror," and he was brother of Avicia, who married Geoffrey, Duke of Brittany.]

(6) **Geoffrey, Avicia.**

(7) **Eudo** — Duke of Brittany.
Married Agnes, daughter of Alan, and died in 1079.

(8) **Ribald** — Lord of Middleham.
[Brother to Alan Rufus, Duke of Richmond, and to Stephen and to Bardolf.] Married Beatrix, and spent his last days in retirement at St. Mary's Abbey, York.

(9) **Randolph** — Lord of Middleham.
Married Agatha, daughter of the first Robert of Bruce.

(10) **Robert Fitz Randolph** — Lord of Middleham.
Who built the Castle of Middleham and married Helewisa de Glanville.

(11) **Randolph Fitz Randolph** — Lord of Middleham.
Married Mary, daughter of Roger Bigot, Duke of Norfolk.

(12) **Randolph Fitz Randolph** — Lord of Middleham.
Who married Anastasia, daughter of William, Lord Percy.

(13) **Mary Fitz Randolph**.
Daughter of Randolph and Anastasia, a rich, religious and benevolent woman who married Robert de Neville. She died A.D. 1320, having survived her husband 49 years.

(14) **Randolph de Neville** — Lord of Middleham.
Whose second wife was Margaret, daughter of Marmaduke Thweng. Died 1332.

(15) **Randolph de Neville** — Lord of Middleham.
Who married Alicia, daughter of Hugo de Audley. Died 1368.

(16) **John de Neville** — Lord of Middleham.
Who married Matilda Percy. [1] Died 1389.

(17) **Randolph de Neville** — Lord of Middleham and first Earl of Westmoreland. Whose first wife was Margaret (daughter of Hugo), Lady Stafford — descended from Edward I — and whose second wife was Joan of Beaufort, daughter of John of Gaunt and granddaughter of Edward III. He died in 1435. By his second wife his posterity runs into and adown the English royal line. See page 36. We now follow the posterity of the Earl of Westmoreland by his first wife, Lady Stafford.

(18) **John** (the children of whose brother Randolph were all daughters) married Elizabeth, daughter of Thomas Holland, Earl of Canterbury. He died two years before his father, in 1433.

(19) **John,** heir presumptive [2] to the dukedom of Westmoreland. Was hero of the battle of Towton, in the year 1461, and bravely lost his life there on the Lancastrian side. He had married Anna, the widow of John de Neville.

(20) **Randolph** — Duke of Westmoreland.

(Son of John and Anna) married Margaret, daughter of Booth de Barton of Lancaster.

(21) **Randolph,** heir presumptive.

Died during his father's lifetime; married Edith, daughter of the Earl of Sandwich.

(22) **Randolph** — Duke of Westmoreland.

(Son of Randolph and Edith), married Catherine, daughter of Edward, Duke of Buckingham. [3] Died 1524.

(23) **Randolph** — fifth son of Randolph and Catherine.

The first son being Henry, whose son Charles was the last in the line of these dukes of Westmoreland, and the other sons being Thomas, Edward, Christopher and Cuthbert. Died probably about 1565.

(24) **Christopher Fitz Randolph** (son of Randolph, fifth son of Duke of Westmoreland).

Married Joan, daughter and heiress of Cuthbert Langton of Langton Hall. Died 1588.

(25) **Edward Fitz Randolph** of Langton Hall.

With whom was found and in whom was confirmed by the "Visitation" of 1614 the Fitz Randolph Arms substantially as borne by the Lords of Middleham and by the Spennithorne branch of Fitz Randolph. Died probably about 1635.

(26) **Edward Fitz Randolph** — Pilgrim.

Married May 10, 1637, at Scituate, Mass., to Elizabeth Blossom, daughter of Thomas and Anne Blossom. Moved to Piscataway, N. J., 1669. Died 1675.

[1] The second of this noble family to become allied with the Neville-Fitz Randolph line.

[2] Hume speaks of him as duke in fact at the time of the battle, and of his being slain with the great Percy, Duke of Northumberland, and a near kinsman, and with Sir John Neville, brother of Westmoreland, and Dacres, another kinsman.

[3] This Buckingham was descended from Thomas Woodstock, Duke of Gloucester, uncle to Richard II. By this pedigree, he was not only allied to the royal family, but had claims tor high dignities and extensive estates. Hume says Buckingham's mother was a daughter of Edmund, Duke of Somerset, descended from Edward III, and mentions "the power and splendor of his family." He was at first a partisan and then an enemy of Richard III.

Chapter Ten - Fitz Randolph Principles and Later Fortunate Alliances

In considering the fact of Edward Fitz Randolph's emigration to Massachusetts, the question arises as to the particular impelling motive for a departure so radical. A certain aggregation of notes or memoranda, occasionally spoken of as Nathaniel Fitz Randolph's Record (made probably in the second generation following the arrival of the Pilgrims) indicate that young Edward's father came with him to the New World. Supposing this statement to be correct, we ask, Why did they come? There is hardly more than one answer that could be given to such a question. Not long afterward, divers persons came (from the Old World to the New) simply to better their fortunes, and such as these have continued to come ever since, and in increasing numbers; but aside perhaps from the sufferings of their family under Tudor rule, still fresh and harrowing to the recollection, there was practically but one influence guiding the Fitz Randolph steps, and it was the same influence that guided the steps of all the American immigrants of the first three decades of the seventeenth century, and *that was Religion.* It was the settled purpose to enjoy liberty of conscience and an untrammeled communion with the Heavenly Father that determined these sturdy citizens of the British Motherland to seek a land (though of a climate of doubtful hospitality) in which might be established a broader and freer citizenship. [1] This earlier emigration included not a few persons in whom high principle and piety were united with a good degree of education and social position, as well as of ability and courage. It is true that of those who fled from, or struggled with, prelatical power and kingly oppression, many were of the lower social rank; but, commingled with these, and holding fraternal relations with them, were English gentlemen and the sons of gentlemen whose blood had descended for centuries from titled families.

If we were disposed to proceed on a line of thought and theory growing out of the emigration of the Fitz Randolphs we would have no difficulty in associating earlier religious affinities with the later religious developments of this family. We have seen how for many hundreds of years their religious character and loyalty had been sustained and continued. From the days of the Norman Conquest, and afterward through the ages that followed, the Fitz Randolphs had generously and even lavishly contributed to Christian causes and charities, establishing monasteries, churches, and hospitals without pause or stint. In the fourteenth century it would appear that this family was socially and otherwise identified with the great movement toward religious freedom which eventuated in the publication of the Wycliffe Bible. Wycliffe was under the protection of John of

Gaunt, whose descendants were the kings of the House of Lancaster, and also of the Earl of Northumberland, Lord Henry Percy, a devoted Lancastrian; so the Lancastrians were inclined to be Lollards, or advocates of Bible reading, and were opposed to extremes of papal power and practices.

Cicely, descendant of Mary Fitz Randolph of Middleham, married Richard Plantagenet, Duke of York; and their children, as we have seen, were Edward IV and Richard III, kings of the House of York. Elizabeth, daughter of Edward IV and granddaughter of Cicely, married, as has been noted, Henry VII, a Lancastrian descendant of John of Gaunt; and thus were combined the houses of York and Lancaster in the person of their son, Henry VIII, and thus an end was definitely made to the Wars of the Roses.

The Lollard leaven was ever at work, and to the thoughtful student of history it will appear that the Open Bible, as opposed to priestly bigotry and restriction, found friends in the fifteenth and sixteenth centuries amongst the intelligent and thoughtful members of the powerful families of Britain; and the seed thus sown developed afterwards not so much indeed in the breaking away of the English Church from Roman Catholicism (which in some sense was a private enterprise of Henry VIII, carried out for his own purposes), [2] as in the more significant separation from the established church in the sixteenth and seventeenth centuries, in which last separation even many thoughtful and conscientious members of noble families participated. These are facts which fit naturally with the emigration to America of families of the Fitz Randolph type; and it is hardly possible to avoid the surmise and the inference that the making of common cause by the men of patrician blood with the plain people who had come to the point of sacrificing their all in the cause of an Open Bible, was in keeping with the traditions of a noble line whose ancestors in the fourteenth century had supported the outspoken father of religious liberty, John Wycliffe.

Young Edward, the emigrant, kept in close touch with the advanced religious thought of those with whom he had embarked his fortune and his life. Some time following the formation of a non-conformist religious society and the establishment of a regular pastorate of the same, Edward joined this society or church. Its pastor was Rev. John Lothrop, who came to Massachusetts a little later than young Edward, and who was an earnest preacher of those days, having been pastor for eight years of a non-conformist society, worshiping secretly in London. Upon his meetings being discovered in 1632 in London, preacher and parishioners were imprisoned for something more than two years. They were released upon Mr. Lothrop's pledging himself to leave the kingdom. So soon as the prison doors were opened for him, he embarked (in the year 1634) in the ship "Griffin" accompanied by thirty of his parishioners. They settled at Scituate, and established a church there January 18, 1635. The following quaint entries in the original style and orthography of Pastor Lothrop himself are copied from his church register: -

Marryed
Edward Fittsrandolfe
May 10, 1637
Elizabeth Blossoms

Edward Fitts Surrandolph
joyned church May 14, 1637
Scituate

Our Brother Fittsrendolfe
wife joyned August 27, 1643
Barnstable.

Incidentally it will be noted that here, in the handwriting of a preacher and a leader of men, are several new and distinct ways of spelling the old Norse name, which for eight hundred years prior to Pastor Lothrop's Records was undergoing numerous odd and curious changes in the course of the centuries, and yet was always susceptible of being traced and identified and even kept in the line of historical narrative.

The Pilgrim, Edward, became very soon a factor of importance. He was a man of substance as well as of character. Mr. Leonard quotes from Pastor Lothrop's diary the statement that "Master Fitzrandolphe" built a house in Scituate during 1636; and it appears that he sold his property there in 1639 and moved to Barnstable with his minister and twenty-five townsmen. Here he built another home on an eight-acre-lot and lived in it till 1649, when he sold it (and three other town lots) and removed to his farm in West Barnstable — a tract of 143 acres. This he occupied for twenty years — when he sold out and moved with his family to Piscataway, N. J. This important change seems to have been brought about (like that from England) by a desire for ampler religious freedom. The augmenting restrictions and exactions of Puritan rule in New England seemed oppressive and unscriptural to a considerable body of excellent men and women who longed for a large liberty of thought. Religious freedom, complete and unstinted, was promised to new settlers by the New Jersey Proprietors, and this constituted the chief lure to the pious pilgrims.

We now arrive at a point in this history and line of tradition at which some special consideration should be given to an alliance with another branch of Pilgrim stock. In the ages gone by the Fitz Randolphs were from time to time exceedingly fortunate in their marriages, gathering increase of strength and character and standing — as well as of wealth — from a number of these alliances. It may safely be said, however, that in no instance of this sort did greater advantage accrue to him who made the contract than was gained by the young Edward who in May, 1637, at Scituate, Mass., married Elizabeth, the daughter of Thomas and Anne Blossom.

Elizabeth Blossom was born in Leyden, Holland, of pious Pilgrim parentage about the year 1620. Her father, Thomas Blossom, was a prominent member of Rev. John Robinson's church from the time its members left Scrooby in Nottinghamshire, Eng. In 1620 the "Mayflower" and the "Speedwell" were to sail as companion ships for America. The "Speedwell" was a little ship of sixty tons, which had been purchased and fitted out in Holland for the Pilgrim congregation. She sailed July 26, 1620, from the port of Delfthaven, about twenty-four miles from Leyden, for Southampton in England, where the "Mayflower" for a week had been waiting with a partial list of passengers from London. It was found that the little "Speedwell" needed repairs before putting out to sea. Repairs were made at considerable expense and delay. The two vessels then set sail for their long voyage, but the "Speedwell" proved leaky and both vessels put into Dartmouth for further repairs. Then once more they sailed together and progressed some three hundred miles westward from Land's End, when the captain of the "Speedwell" complained further of his boat's unseaworthiness. Again the two vessels turned back, this time putting into Plymouth harbor, and here it was decided to dismiss the "Speedwell" after a redistribution of passengers and cargo.

Referring to this event, Governor Bradford wrote — "So, after they had took out such provision as the other ship could well stow, and concluded what number and what persons to send back, they made another sad parting, the little ship (the "Speedwell") going to London, and the other (the "Mayflower") proceeding on her voyage."

This grievous and discouraging work was performed by September 6, 1620, and eighteen persons returned in the "Speedwell" to Leyden by way of London, where the leaky boat was sold. Among those returning was Thomas Blossom — with his little family. He, with a few other leading Pilgrims, accompanied the despondent passengers back to their church-friends in Holland. Here he remained with Pastor Robinson, who continued to shepherd the flock until such time as the Society was able to send over to America others of the congregation.

Two such embarkations took place prior to the death of the pious old preacher in 1625, and the remaining members embarked in subsequent voyages about 1630. The ship "Fortune" in November, 1621, brought over twenty-five members of the church besides children; and in August, 1623, the "Ann" and "Little James" carried across sixty more church-members in addition to children.

The Pilgrim church in Leyden and its transported membership at New Plymouth in America continued as one body. The branch in the New World never chose a pastor so long as Pastor Robinson was living. During the interim Elder Brewster presided over the spiritual concerns of the struggling congregation at Cape Cod until 1629. He had been one of the foremost pioneers in the Nottinghamshire movement in England, which resulted in establishing the Separatists' Society in 1607. From 1589 to September, 1607, he had been postmaster at Scrooby by appointment from Sir Thomas Randolph, Comptroller of all Her Majesty's Posts.

After Pastor Robinson died, in 1625, Thomas Blossom wrote sorrowfully to Governor Bradford of this event and of the distress of the church, and strenuous efforts were put forth by the Pilgrim congregation to bring over to America the remainder of the parent Society in Leyden. [3] So soon as they were able to arrange payment of their obligations to the organized "Adventurers" in England, and buy out their interest in the Pilgrim colony in New England, they began to bring over the remainder of the brethren — though at great cost, sacrifice and anxiety.

"Thomas Blossom came over to Plymouth, probably in 1629, and was chosen a deacon of the church. Bradford speaks of him as one of 'our ancient friends in Holland.' The church records describe him as 'a holy man and experienced saint,' and 'competently accomplished with abilities for his place.' He died in the summer of 1633." [Plym. Ch. Rec. i. 42, and Prince's Annals, p. 437.]

On May 1, 1629, six vessels left the shores of England with a passenger list which included the bulk of the Leyden congregation, all bound for New England. One of these ships appears to have been the famous "Mayflower;" and included among its passengers were Pastor Robinson's widow and children; and it is believed that Thomas Blossom and his family were also among the passengers of this same vessel. It is certain that they came over in 1629. He was one of the first deacons of the Pilgrim Church in Plymouth after his arrival in the Colony, and continued in that office so long as he lived. After the death of Deacon Blossom, in 1633, his widow joined the church at Scituate. In 1639 the family moved with Pastor Lothrop from Scituate to Barnstable. Edward Fitz Randolph had joined the church in 1637 at Scituate. His wife (as has been seen) joined it half a dozen years later at Barnstable. She attained the age of ninety-three in her later home in New Jersey. The aroma of a fine Christian character has ever surrounded the memory of this beloved and venerated woman. Her children and her children's children for many generations have risen up to call her blessed. She came with her family from Massachusetts to New Jersey in 1669; and near the spot where the peaceful Raritan finds the sea her soul went out to the Eternal and Divine Peace.

And what shall we say of other commingling of family histories and characteristics? Coming down from remotest ages are kindred elements and influences ever seeking to mate with each other — though unconsciously — and eventually embracing and joining their forces for the world's benefit. The noble and gentle blood of the Fownes was not, for a century after the visit of the American Pilgrims to Plymouth, joined with the mingled blood of the Fitz Randolphs and the Blossoms in any human veins; yet in spirit these families were striving toward like ends. Whilst Thomas Fownes was Mayor of Plymouth, Eng., the Pilgrims found in him a staunch and influential friend. With his offspring was soon allied a family equally noble and strong — that of the Winthrops — a family that furnished for the enterprising infant colonies of New England a line of grand and able governors reaching through successive generations; and this united blood of the Fownes and Winthrops went on its way of purity, simplicity, ability and self-denial (and betimes under the modest Quaker garb worn by the Feakes, the Bownes, the Thornes and the Laings) to join the ancient clan of the Edgars [4] and the worthy lineage of the Mannings, and in due course to find and be amalgamated with the heirs of all the Fitz Randolph traditions and purposes in their now settled home in New Jersey. [5]

Meantime startling questions had arisen between the Colonies and the Motherland; and some of the Fitz Randolphs, whose fathers had fought for the Motherland in Canada in the controversies in which good Queen Anne became involved with the French, felt compelled to stand with their neighbors in asserting manhood rights against King George's arbitrary dictates. Against these unreasonable dictates Quaker blood, as well as Baptist and Puritan and Pilgrim blood rebelled; and those who buckled on armor in defence of what they considered human rights acquitted themselves bravely and well. As to all the stories of more recent years, including the still greater and more terrible strife of "the sixties," when American fought American in the contest of Union versus Disunion, and as to all the bravery and statesmanship developed out of that fierce contest, are they not all written — together with the participation therein of our Fitz Randolph family — in the books of service, the State Records and the histories of our own age, and of the age not long since closed?

Our country is still making important history every day, and it may at least be modestly hoped that on each of its pages may be found a record not wholly dissociated from the spirit of energy and high and worthy purpose which has hitherto pervaded our Fitz Randolph traditions.

[1] It will be borne in mind that the Stuarts had succeeded the Tudors and had fairly out-Tudored the Tudors in forcing the state religion, as established by Henry VIII, alike on the old Catholics of Yorkshire and on the Presbyterians of Scotland.

[2] No disrespect on the part of the writer is, or could be, intended toward the English church of the twentieth century, or toward its offspring and comrade in work — the Episcopal Church of America. The course of Providence is alike mysterious and beneficent. Out of imperfect ideals noble results have developed. Even out of evil, good has come; and our hearts still beat in time with the footstep of Divine progress.

[3] See Young's Chronicles, pp. 480-8. Thomas Blossom's letter to the governor is dated at Leyden, Dec. 16, 1626. Its closing lines are as below:

"I commend you to the keeping of the Lord, desiring, if He see it good (and that I might be serviceable unto the business) that I were with you. Cod hath taken away my son, that was with me in the ship, when I went back again; I have only two children, which were born since I left you. Fare you well." One of these two children was Elizabeth, destined wife of Edward Fitz Randolph.

[4] Descended from Cospatric, son of Maldred by Algetha, daughter and heiress of Uchtred, Prince of Northumbria by Elfgiva, daughter of King Ethelred. This was the source also from which the Nevilles, or Fitz Maldreds, sprung. See "Genealogical Collections concerning the Scottish House of Edgar," published by the Grampian Club in 1878.

[5] It is also noteworthy that the descendants of the liberal and hospitable Hollanders, with whom the Pilgrims of the seventeenth century found an

asylum — with conscience-freedom-— should, within the last hundred years become allied by family ties with the descendants of those whom their fathers had succored and protected. See Histories of Van Syckel and Opdyke families.

Milton Keynes UK
Ingram Content Group UK Ltd.
UKHW010629290424
441924UK00001B/128